Praise for STRONG

'Simplicity is the real power of STRONG. Whilst many of the concepts within the book are not new, Anna has presented them in a simple yet meaningful way for anyone involved in sales (which is technically everyone!). With its foundations in positive psychology, this book provides readers with strategies to increase their team's engagement, performance and productivity and enhance their own careers.'

—*Sam Tremethick, Chief Retail and Partnerships Officer, AIA Australia*

'Anna says, "Sales leaders, your role is to support your people, help them grow and develop, and trust them to achieve what's expected. You motivate, inspire, guide and coach them to be their best." She's right.

This outstanding book provides a recipe for leadership success described through stories that resonate, practical examples and easy-to-follow guidelines. STRONG is more than an acronym: Strengths, Trust and Psychological Safety, Resilience, Optimism, Networks, and Goals and Purpose are all key elements of success in building an environment where everyone thrives and sales success follows. STRONG is an essential read for all leaders, particularly those leading sales teams.'

—*Ron Hooton, CEO, Vision Australia*

'STRONG is a must-read for every sales leader looking to improve team performance and create a thriving, high-performing workplace culture. Anna's storytelling, supported by evidence-based strategies, is refreshingly easy to absorb and keeps us craving the next chapter. The STRONG principles combine the key attributes that sales leaders and teams can adopt to improve results significantly. I highly recommend this book to all sales leaders wanting to shift the performance dial in the right direction!'

—*Rob Joyes, State Chief Executive-Victoria, Colliers International*

'Leadership can be hard, but leading an underperforming sales team is one of the toughest gigs to find yourself in. Is it you, your team, or your organisation that needs to change, and how? STRONG is full of hacks on where to look for answers and practical tips to flip you from struggling to thriving. Anna has beautifully woven many of today's most prominent concepts and theories from the genres of leadership and peak performance, saving you valuable time so that you can immediately start becoming a stronger sales leader.'

—*Brad Fox, Managing Director, SmartBrave Consulting*

'As a sales book, STRONG is a completely different read. Rather than focusing on skill, process and productivity, it gets you thinking about how the whole team performs and how your ability as a leader can directly affect your team's success. Focusing on leadership rather than the team, leaves us wanting to know more and to learn how to create and keep successful sales teams. STRONG over SWOT – find the positive and focus on the strengths.'

—*David Colman, Director, PRD*

'An intelligent yet simplified mix of experience, research, science and collective wisdom synthesised in the cleverly chosen acronym STRONG. This framework supports sales leaders to identify areas of focus and attention, and to rise to new levels of engagement, accomplishment and repeatable success, or as the book describes – to thrive. Even successful leaders can use the concepts described and address the challenges captured within the stories. I found myself motivated by the ideas.'

—*Peter Gommers, Senior Leader, Financial Services*

'This book is exactly what we need to excel at selling today. STRONG challenges traditional thinking by focusing on what unlocks our sales potential. You'll learn that results come through honing people skills, not just mastering scripts or following protocols, and discover the power of tapping into individual and collective motivations as the key to enhancing performance. In this new era of selling, where being human is a superpower, STRONG provides the intel to improve leadership and sales results at all levels. Sales doesn't feel so hard when you look at it from this perspective.'

—*Kim Payne, speaker, trainer and coach*

'For leaders wanting to impact performance and see their teams thrive in challenging environments, STRONG provides a solid starting point. With off-field skills impacting results as much as technical sales techniques, STRONG has a footing in research that shows the cost and opportunity of attending to these skills. Much will resonate with seasoned sales leaders. Anna's book includes easily applied frameworks, exercises and tools that detail the range of STRONG principles. New leaders will recognise what makes a high performing team and have practical tools to accelerate their leadership success. Presented in an accessible, easy-to-read format, the STRONG principles are an excellent guide for any sales leader.'

— *Tamara Joyner, Regional Vice President Sales*

'Sales leaders will enjoy STRONG. It's concise, well-structured and research-based, reinforcing the principles and providing confidence that this approach will work. New managers will benefit from this book as a source to rely on. For those more experienced, it's a good reminder of the areas they should focus on but may have been forgotten. The book outlines practical strategies to implement, which makes it really easy for sales leaders to apply and take action immediately. STRONG is a great framework to plan your sales year and continue to use to check in and ensure you're still on track.'

— *Eric Fransella, Enterprise Account Executive, Zendesk*

'STRONG is the book I needed 12 years ago when the opportunity to lead sales people presented itself. Fortunately for you, it's here. Leading energy-driven deal hunters is like navigating a maze with no map. STRONG gives you the tools you require, the confidence that "you can do this" and the conviction that "you're doing it right and doing right by the people you lead".'

—*Tom Hayes, Senior Director, CBRE*

STRONG

STRONG

ANNA GLYNN

How the best sales leaders
engage, achieve and thrive

Published by Anna Glynn

First published in 2024 in Melbourne, Australia

Copyright © Anna Glynn

www.annaglynn.com.au

Edited by Jenny Magee

Typeset and printed in Australia by BookPOD

ISBN: 978-0-9756490-0-8 (paperback)
ISBN: 978-0-9756490-1-5 (ebook)

CONTENTS

*Being a salesperson isn't just something to do;
it's someone to be.*

ACKNOWLEDGEMENTS

This book has not been written alone. Many amazing people have supported me along the way.

Thank you to my book coach, Kelly Irving, for her early guidance and support on the book structure and the Expert Author Community for providing advice. Thank you to Jenny Magee for her brilliant editing, and Sylvie Blair and the BookPOD team for their production and publishing expertise.

I am grateful for the Thought Leaders Business School community, who inspire and encourage me to achieve what I never thought possible.

My thanks to David Colman, Brad Fox, Eric Fransella, Peter Gommers, Tom Hayes, Ron Hooton, Tamara Joyner, Kim Payne and Sam Tremethick who provided input and feedback on early iterations, and all the other sales leaders who regularly let me pick their brains.

Thank you to Michelle McQuaid and Paige Williams, two incredible mentors, who challenge me to expand and whose work and thinking I admire.

Thank you to the incredible researchers on whose shoulders this book stands. These include Ed Deci, Jane Dutton, Amy Edmondson, BJ Fogg, Barbara Fredrickson, Alex Linley, Ann Masten, Marie-Gabrielle Reed, Richard Ryan, Peter Schulman, Marty Seligman and Mike Steger. The list goes on and includes all those from whom I have learned in the positive psychology community.

Thank you to my clients. I have tested these strategies on them and their stories are captured in this book. I have learnt so much from them.

Finally, thank you to Rob and Tommy, who support, encourage, love and believe in me – there's no better feeling in the world!

PREFACE

I am fortunate to have spent a large part of my life in sales.

I dipped my toe into this wonderful world by selling homemade goods from the side of the road with my best friend. At eight years of age, we convinced passers-by that a jar of water with a lavender twig was the latest perfume they absolutely had to have.

Many years later, fresh out of university, I landed my first corporate role in sales, an area that just seemed to fit. My education never taught me about sales, yet I found myself doing work that felt great. I loved (and still do) the excitement of engaging with prospects, the sense of achievement when you hit your targets and developing and delivering products and services to meet a client's needs.

Whilst on the front-line, I learnt the *101* of selling – how to prospect, negotiate, listen, influence, identify decision-makers, communicate, close, deal with multiple stakeholders, problem-solve, understand buyer preferences, develop strategy, and build relationships.

As I did well as an individual contributor, I was eventually put into a management position. Yet, perhaps, like you, I had no idea what to do as a team leader. Suddenly, I was responsible for motivating, inspiring and leading my team to deliver (if not exceed) our goals. On top of that, I was in charge of increasing their engagement and looking after their wellbeing. No small feat!

Although I'd attended many incredible training programs over the years and been guided by some excellent mentors and coaches, I felt neither equipped nor confident to deliver what was expected of me. All the sales competencies I had learned couldn't help me overcome my challenges and lead my team to success.

I devoured books, case studies, articles and interviews – anything to build my understanding of what drove workplace engagement, resilience, wellbeing and performance. Organisations had existed for centuries, so surely the answers existed somewhere.

During my research, I discovered positive psychology, which focuses on what leads to thriving people, teams, workplaces, communities and societies. I couldn't believe there was a whole field trying to find answers to everything I wanted to know!

Fortunately, the Centre for Wellbeing Science at the University of Melbourne offers courses and degrees in this space. So, I embarked on a graduate diploma, where I gained new skills and strategies that I tested out with my team. And I saw great results – not just on our scorecards but in our relationships with one another, our motivation, energy and commitment.

I was having an impact, so my confidence to lead grew, even though some of what I was doing differed from how I was led and how my organisation was influencing me to lead. But these new strategies felt right, so I continued.

As the benefits of the positive psychology approach became increasingly obvious, I became hooked on the field and wanted to learn as much as I could. So, a few years later, I signed up for the Masters of Applied Positive Psychology program at Melbourne University.

During my study, I recognised that I was learning everything organisations needed and wanted to know, but it wasn't being taught to leaders or their teams. I decided to launch my own practice, where I could share these strategies with workplaces so they, too, could achieve the outcomes they were after.

Fast forward to today, and I am grateful to work with organisations from all different sectors around the world, sharing what I know and continuing to learn with leaders and their teams. In the simplest terms, I teach everything I wish I had known when I was leading.

My hope in doing this work is that organisations become places where workers can be at their best each day, where they are better for having worked there, where burnout isn't the norm, and where we all achieve more and thrive.

This book captures some of my deepest learning about how to be an outstanding sales leader. These lessons have come from academic studies, yet they've also been shared in interviews with leaders running exceptional sales teams. They've also come from my work testing these strategies with individuals.

My hope is that this book gives other sales leaders the confidence to lead their teams to deeper engagement and impact so they can attain better results and move closer towards thriving in this increasingly complex and ever-changing world.

INTRODUCTION

Nothing happens until a sale is made

– Thomas Watson Snr.

Sales teams are the backbone of every business.

It's incredibly hard for an organisation to survive if they don't hit their targets. And because of this, sales teams are under enormous pressure to deliver.

Yet despite the importance of the role, sales doesn't have an honourable image. You don't hear children saying they want to be a salesperson when they grow up! In his book *To Sell is Human,* Daniel Pink even described sales as the *'white-collar equivalent of cleaning toilets'.*[1] *Ouch!*

Many outsiders mistake the long lunches, client conferences, mid-week dinners and coffee catchups as fun. And sure, some fun does come with the territory, but it's hard work, too. Often really hard work. Much of the effort put in with prospects, sometimes over months or even years, doesn't result in a sale.

It's even harder for sales leaders. They're under pressure to ensure their team delivers as they're ultimately responsible for their teams' performance and success. Yet it's becoming harder to be a successful sales leader, given the growing complexity and challenge of their role. Clients and teams are demanding more from them, the workplace is changing faster than ever, and there is mounting pressure to perform.

Sales teams are exhausted and flailing, and the strategies sales leaders have traditionally used to motivate and engage their teams aren't working. Leaders don't always admit it, but how they lead today won't get them where they need to go.

> How they lead today won't get them where they need to go.

Even though they might be achieving some reasonable outcomes now, these aren't sustainable over the long-term. Their concern is that sales will get harder before they get easier. As their confidence dips, these leaders are beginning to feel they're not cut out for the job. They're questioning whether they're good enough to lead their teams to success and calculating the risks if they don't. That's because, in sales, it's pretty basic; you either hit your targets and know you've done a good job. Or you miss your targets, and you've done a bad job. As a sales leader, missing your targets by a lot might mean no job.

Given all this, it's no wonder many sales leaders are at breaking point. They're tired, frustrated and struggling. They're at risk of burnout – if they're not there already.

The good news, however, is that some sales leaders are doing well, really well, amidst the struggles. They are accomplishing exactly what we all want as leaders. They've taken their leadership to the next level by switching to evidence-backed techniques. They are confident about what needs to be done to engage, achieve and thrive over the long term.

Rather than trying to manage their teams to deliver results using punishments or rewards, they've created an environment where people can do their best work. They and their teams are satisfied, connected, and committed. They take ownership of their performance, cope well with challenges and put in more effort with their colleagues and clients. These teams have a competitive edge and are attractive to talent. And because they're flourishing at work, their personal lives are positively impacted, which is why they are considered the best.

Who is this book for?

This book is for leaders in sales – specifically, five distinct types of sales leaders, although the ideas and strategies will be helpful to all.

The first type are great at sales and great at leading. These leaders excelled as individual contributors during their many years in the field, so naturally, they were promoted and given a sales team to lead. They intuitively do a lot of the things captured in this book. So, they're good sales leaders, but they're not really sure why. If you ask them how they lead, they can't explain and nor can they teach their strategies to others. We want more sales teams like theirs, but the leader doesn't fully understand what they're doing. These leaders need to learn what they're doing and how to teach it to their teams and others.

Next is the leader who is great at sales but terrible at leading. They've been in sales for most, if not all, their careers. Before becoming a leader, they proved they were able to sell successfully. They know how to handle negotiations and knockbacks better than anyone. They show their teams all the ins and outs of selling. Technically, they're brilliant, but they lack many of the skills required to lead their teams to be their best. They're excellent salespeople but, unfortunately, not great leaders.

The third is those who are great at sales but new to leading. They have made the transition from salesperson to manager, which isn't natural for most people. Yet they received little or no leadership training, so they lack the critical skills to manage a team. They have no idea how to recruit, lead, motivate or engage their workers. They feel totally lost as leaders and aren't sure what they should be doing. They see other leaders and their teams doing well and want to learn their strategies.

The fourth group includes leaders who are not great at sales but are impressive at leading. Like the first group, they naturally adopt the strategies in this book and are good sales leaders, but they're not sure what they're doing - even though their team is doing well. They want to learn what they're doing and how to teach it to others.

And finally, there are the sales leaders who don't realise they're in sales. These are all the people who are selling every day but don't consider themselves to be in sales. They may be lawyers, architects, teachers, doctors, accountants, relationship managers or engineers. They're in sales because, in some way, shape or form, their role is to influence or persuade someone to do business with them. They might be on stage encouraging people to change, writing articles, or improving lives or businesses through their expertise. They have something others need, and there's an exchange of value for that. But they don't believe that they *sell* or they are in *sales*. But they are because, as Daniel Pink said, 'to sell is human'.

It's important to point out that when I refer to leadership, it isn't necessarily about someone's title or the number of direct reports they have. Leadership is something we can all choose to do. It's a decision. Even if you aren't in an official management position, you can still be a leader, and this book is for you.

Regardless of your title or which group you identify with, this book will give you the confidence to unleash potential within yourself and your team and create environments where all can thrive.

About this book

By now, you're probably keen to understand what will unfold in the coming pages, so here's an overview of what lies ahead.

Part One examines the challenges facing sales leaders and their teams and why these impede success. We will also make the case for why sales leadership needs to change.

In Part Two, we take a deep dive into evidence-backed strategies that boost engagement, wellbeing, resilience and performance at work. We will uncover why they're necessary for sales leaders to adopt and how they can be actioned.

And finally, Part Three will reveal how we can ensure the changes we want to make will be successful and how to amplify the outcomes we wish to see.

How to use this book

As you work your way through the chapters, you'll encounter stories from the frontline (with names changed) and learn the evidence-backed strategies that empower sales teams to thrive.

I promise you won't be learning yet another sales methodology or technique.

By the end, you'll have the latest science at your fingertips and you'll be armed with a suite of tools you can apply immediately with your team.

> Not only will you have better salespeople, but you'll have better humans, too.

But more than that, you'll have learned more about yourself and your leadership.

By switching to the evidence-backed strategies captured in these pages, you will lead better, do better and be better. Just imagine the impact of this on you and everyone around you. Not only will you have better salespeople, but you'll have better humans, too.

However, good science is never proven. We are always learning more. So, I ask that you experiment with the ideas within this book. Let them test and challenge you. Pull them apart, test them out and see what works best for you and your team.

Let's get started!

PART 1

CHAPTER ONE

THE CHALLENGES OF SALES LEADERS

The world we find ourselves in poses unique and greater challenges than we've ever endured. These hurdles make it increasingly difficult for sales leaders to achieve exceptional outcomes or, in some cases, even the bare minimum.

Regardless of the industry or the size or location of the company, sales leaders are dealing with largely the same challenges.

Most sales leaders I speak with say their biggest current challenge is the retention and attraction of talent. This is backed up by reports from PricewaterhouseCoopers and Development Dimensions International's 2023 CEO Leadership Report.[1, 2] These leaders say they're finding it

> Their biggest current challenge is the retention and attraction of talent.

really tough to recruit quality talent and are working harder than ever to keep their star performers.

Attrition is costly for any team, but a salesperson's turnover is even more so. In addition to the normal costs of non-sales roles, turnover hurts sales teams even more because whilst the roles sit empty or aren't replaced, existing client relationships aren't nurtured or are even neglected. When your salespeople leave, this can kill customer retention. So staff turnover is expensive, sometimes as much as four times the salesperson's pay.[3]

What's more, a sales team's budget typically continues its trajectory each year despite losing head count. When teams don't have adequate resources (people) to meet the demands of their jobs or their workplace requires too much of them, they can feel worn out, leading to burnout.[4] This is worrying because sales teams are being asked to do more with less. That includes people, money and time, particularly whenever there's a looming economic downturn.

Gallup suggests that higher demands on workers could also be contributing to the decrease in engagement seen in Australia and around the world.[5] Employee engagement is a significant driver of job satisfaction and organisational commitment, so the fallout from this trend is costly. Gallup also estimates that staff disengagement costs $3,400 out of every $10,000 worth of salary paid.[6] What's more, employee engagement directly impacts an employee's performance.[7]

Given that 70% of team engagement is attributable to the leader, it's an area in glaring need of fixing.[8]

Sales teams are asking more of their leaders; they want greater flexibility in their role, their wellbeing looked after and for leaders to foster the teams' sense of purpose.[9]

In all, the people side of the sales leader's role is becoming more difficult as they look for ways to engage and motivate their teams to achieve results and develop the next generation of salespeople.

Sales leaders are under increased pressure to perform. This comes from their own leaders as well as from the CEO and the board, as the company's success rests on the sales team delivering on their KPIs.

> The people side of the sales leader's role is becoming more difficult.

Pressure is also stemming from the continued disruption that is present in the market. The business environment is ever-changing and continues to evolve at an unprecedented pace. Constant fluctuations in interest rates, technology advancements, and unexpected emerging competitors are causing much angst for those in sales.

Customer preferences and expectations are constantly shifting and increasing. They want more from their products or services, yet they want to spend less and are willing to go elsewhere to get what they want. It's taking a lot more effort and time to get deals over the line and the pace to close is slowing.

What's more, it's hard to escape the pressure as it's felt in their personal lives too. With the cost of living increasing, sales leaders are under significant stress at home as their families' livelihoods also rely on their success. So, the pressure is coming from several different directions and can't be avoided.

Given the challenges, it's no wonder sales stress is at an all-time high. Many salespeople are exhausted, seriously struggling or burning out. Sales teams aren't convinced they can deliver on their KPIs against such a tough backdrop. The stress they're experiencing also hurts their performance and productivity. As a result, they become more disengaged, demotivated, and dissatisfied with their roles. It's not surprising that many are actively seeking new jobs.[10]

> If they don't succeed, their jobs, reputations, careers and livelihoods are on the line.

These challenges are making it hard for sales leaders to do their job. Their confidence to support their teams to overcome these hurdles and achieve what's expected is dipping.

They're unsure how to lead their teams to success, yet if they don't succeed, their jobs, reputations, careers and livelihoods are on the line.

Why aren't sales leaders ready to overcome these challenges?

Training and development should be a strategic imperative in every workplace. Many organisations know this and spend a lot of time and money on training their teams – particularly their sales divisions.

According to the Association for Talent Development, workplaces invest, on average, over US$1000 to US$1500 per year per salesperson on sales training.[11] That amounts to more than US$100 billion each year.[12] However, sales training typically focuses on the basics of *how* to sell.[13] These include handling objections, making calls, influencing, building pipelines, negotiating, listening, communicating, stakeholder management, buyer preferences and relationship building.

These factors build a salesperson's aptitude – just what they need when they go out and sell.

Often, this training teaches the latest sales methodology that promises to make a salesperson successful. It might be SPIN selling (Situation, Problem, Implication, Need-payoff), needs-based selling, barrier selling, psychological selling, mood selling, customer-centric selling, solution selling, or (my favourite) the science in selling, where you observe the shape of your prospect's skull to learn more about their character.[14]

> No sales methodology has proved more successful than any other.

Yet despite the plethora of options, no sales methodology has proved more successful than any other in defeating challenges and boosting sales performance. And they aren't typically aimed at driving team engagement, resilience or wellbeing.

Don't get me wrong, a sales methodology absolutely has a place in sales training, particularly for those who might be new to the role, and you can always learn something to add to your sales toolkit. But rarely does sales training teach everything else that sales leaders and their people need to know so they can thrive. For instance, these programs don't typically teach people how to overcome hurdles, be at their best or build a team that retains and attracts the best sales talent.

What about leadership training?

In addition to annual sales training, most organisations spend much of their budget on leadership training.

Like sales methodologies, leadership training also tends to focus on the latest management theory (servant, courageous, transformational, authentic, ethical, etc.) that offers fresh ideas on how best to lead a team. But what's taught isn't always effective as it fails to translate into the workplace. Leadership theories lack evidence or do not equate with the results we're after.

> Leadership theories lack evidence or do not equate with the results we're after.

It's hard to know which management theory or style is best for our current challenges. Which will help us be more engaged or create cultures that attract quality talent. Most training programs are off-the-shelf, so they're not always the right fit for a team. And some are rarely updated, so they don't address current or immediate issues.

Yet some organisations don't provide leadership training to their employees at all. They don't invest in their leaders because they believe that being an effective individual contributor means they can manage their teams effectively.

> ## Leadership requires a set of learned skills.

Yet the skills required to be a good salesperson are not the same as being a good or even great sales leader. Some think that people should be able to lead based on instinct. But it isn't something we're born with; leadership requires a set of learned skills and many leaders long for instruction on which approach to follow.

What's more, not upskilling leaders can have disastrous effects on teams.

Of course, learning how to lead doesn't just come from the classroom; we can gain experience from other leaders around us. But their approaches might not resonate with you. Nor deliver the outcomes you seek.

Trained or not, many sales leaders aren't (or don't feel) equipped with the critical capabilities and skills to survive and thrive in this world.

Summary

- Sales teams are one of the most important divisions of organisations.
- Sales leaders are ultimately responsible for the success of their teams.
- The challenges of sales leaders have never been greater or more difficult.
- Many sales leaders aren't confident and have not been properly trained to lead their teams to success.

CHAPTER TWO

MIND THE GAP

Sales leaders and researchers have long been interested in how to improve results, given how important this is for organisations to survive. Over the decades, some answers have emerged.

Positive psychology, in particular, has uncovered how to boost engagement, resilience, wellbeing and performance and prevent workplace burnout. These strategies include playing to strengths, adopting a growth mindset, being optimistic, understanding purpose, building high-quality connections and being resilient. These approaches lead individuals, teams and organisations to reach their goals and more.

In sport we would call these the 'off-field' factors, the activities focused on that help players to be better 'on-field'. This is the work that is done when no

How to *be* a salesperson, as opposed to how to *do* sales.

one is watching. They're about how to *be* a salesperson, as opposed to how to *do* sales, that help us to achieve greater results that can be sustained over the long term. Here, we are talking about adopting the right mindset, using our internal resources like strengths to bring out our best, or our coping skills to overcome hurdles. Or developing great relationships that can support us in good and bad times. Or how you stay motivated to achieve your goals in an increasingly difficult environment. These are the skills that deliver 'on-field' success.

We've seen plenty of examples of organisations achieving success by focusing on these strategies. In the corporate sector, these include Xero, KPMG, Accenture, Swisse, Vision Australia, Medibank Private, Australia Post, McDonald's, PEXA, NSW Ambulance, and Bendigo and Adelaide Bank. We've also seen sporting teams achieve more by adopting these principles, including the Richmond Football Club, the Matildas, Cricket Australia and Melbourne Victory. And our children are learning these principles at school, too.

Yet, despite being known and shown to work, these strategies haven't yet been fully incorporated into the sales arena. These skills aren't typically featured as a fundamental component of sales training and they're not found in the sales literature. Nor do they feature heavily on conference agendas.

Perhaps these skills have been (or still are) considered 'soft' because they focus somewhat on people being happier and healthier. Maybe they require more effort and time to adapt. Or they may go against traditional command-and-control leadership styles.

So, we need to close the gap between what research has uncovered and what's being done by sales leaders. We need a different approach. Something that works to end rising disengagement, stress and burnout, and equips sales leaders to lead their teams to success.

When sales leaders update their skills, they create conditions for better engagement, resilience, performance and wellbeing. The priority remains and will always be on long-term sustainable results; we're just changing the strategies used to get there.

We need a different approach.

What happens when this change is made?

We've accepted the need for change. What happens when this change is made? And how does it show up in your work?

To understand that, I've developed the ladder in Figure 1, outlining the five typical states salespeople experience from burning out to thriving.

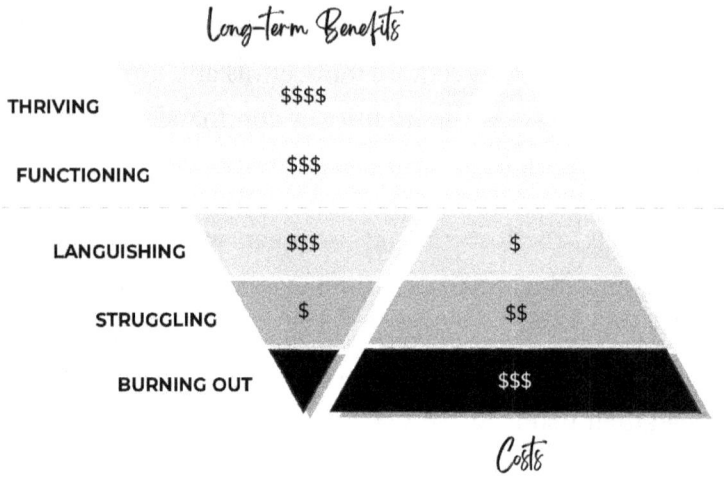

Figure 1: Burning out to Thriving ladder

Over half of our teams are operating above the line.

My research indicates that over half of our teams are operating above the line, either *functioning* or *thriving*.

These teams have leaders who are confidently leading their teams to success. They do whatever it takes to keep their teams above the line. These leaders greatly impact everyone around them, and their teams look to them for the behaviours they should adopt and how they should approach things. They ensure that their teams are engaged and motivated, experience time in flow, have a strong understanding of their purpose, have high-quality team relationships and have strategies to cope with challenges.

Because of this, these teams have lifted their average. They perform better and achieve more. They're more engaged, with greater resilience, increased wellbeing, less stress, burnout and turnover. Their work strengthens rather than depletes them. As a result, they're more satisfied with their roles and more committed to their workplace.

Given the state of their teams and the workplace culture, the leaders are more energised and motivated and less exhausted and stressed. They receive positive feedback from their teams and their leaders, reinforcing their approach. The organisation is pleased as the team outcomes directly impact the bottom line. There are fewer sick days and compensation claims and greater productivity and performance. There is lower turnover and the organisation is more attractive to quality talent. These leaders are admired within their workplace and their industry. They make it look easy and others want to learn from them. They are role models because they have achieved what others want.

Leaders who feel good and function well take this home with them. When they're at their best, this positively impacts their families and their communities.

If more than half of teams are above the line, that leaves just under half languishing, struggling or at burnout. These teams are typically led by leaders who aren't confident in their approach. They know where their teams are but aren't sure how to help them improve. Their efforts have minimal impact, as they use old management techniques that aren't creating change. They're ignoring the off-field factors.

As a result, their teams struggle to focus on what's important. They're less motivated and engaged due to the increased stress they're experiencing, which impacts their performance and productivity. They scramble to complete tasks, typically make more mistakes and have more accidents. They're not equipped to cope well with the challenges that arise, so they feel exhausted. Those feelings negatively impact their relationships at work and provide little connection to their organisation's purpose. Because of this, they become cynical about work and even consider leaving their roles. Emotions spread like wildfire, so if a few team members feel this way, it can quickly spread throughout entire teams.

Teams that operate below the line experience greater stress, less engagement, decreased wellbeing and resilience; as a result, they see more burnout and turnover. The organisation's reputation can suffer if these challenges are known externally.

Reflecting team morale, leaders are highly stressed about what the future holds and feel lost and depleted. There's not a lot of benefit from operating here – apart from, of course, the opportunity to improve.

In the short term, it can be argued that you can still achieve your KPIs when you're operating below the line, but that is not sustainable over the long term. Chances are, even though you are performing well, you'll be exhausted, stressed, and on the path to burnout. And this will impact those around you, including your loved ones.

Why is there so much focus on leaders?

I've written this book for sales leaders because they impact their teams more than any other factor. Leaders influence team productivity, the ability to deliver on outcomes and the capacity to thrive.

Your role is to support your people, help them grow and develop, and trust them to achieve what's expected. You motivate, inspire, guide and coach them to be their best. When interviewing people in sales, I ask who their sales idols are. The majority mention their current or previous leader. Learning from that person had a far greater impact on their development than any sales training they had been on. Are you that person for someone?

When leaders set a great example, teams are more likely to follow and do well.

Workers look to their leaders for mentorship, for examples

of how to approach particular scenarios and what to do in their day-to-day. When leaders set a great example, teams are more likely to follow and do well. Remember that you shape the experience your people have at work. If you micromanage teams, pit them against one another, or belittle or distrust them, they won't have a good experience or quality relationship with you, which may encourage them to leave. Poor leadership is often cited as one of the main drivers of turnover.[1]

Organisations need leaders to set the tone for the behaviours they wish to see. You are the first step in engineering the culture they want. When you act in a way that is not aligned with your team or organisation's values, this sends a clear message that this isn't important.

Ultimately, salespeople with exceptional leaders are engaged, achieve more and thrive.

Where are you at?

Now that we've described how leaders and teams experience and impact each other, it's time to find out where you are at.

- Where would you place yourself on the 'Burning out to Thriving' ladder?
- Where are most of your team? Is this different from you? Why?
- What are the long-term benefits and costs of this?

- Where do you want to be?
- Where do you want your team to be?

Please know that the aim isn't to have your whole team consistently thriving. That isn't achievable, given the constant challenges in our professional and personal lives. What's more, our emotional state ebbs and flows depending on what's happening around us. Thriving isn't the final destination; it's an ongoing journey.

Thriving isn't the final destination; it's an ongoing journey.

The goal here is to give sales leaders tools so they and their teams can thrive. That means they are equipped with strategies for when things aren't going so well.

Don't just guess what state your team is in. Research and experience tell us we're not very good at reading other people's minds. We usually get it wrong. So, if you're unsure where your team is at, the best thing you can do is ask.

If you're in a better position than your team, this may be due to the greater autonomy and flexibility that comes with a leadership role.

If your team is higher on the ladder than you are, this might reflect the increased pressure and challenges you face. This can make it harder for the team to thrive over the long term. The flight risk for the team is higher, given that people tend to leave jobs because of their leader.

These questions may have uncovered a gap between where you and your team are and where you want to be. The next part of this book will outline strategies to help you close that gap.

However, you may have discovered that you and your team are in the right place. The next part of the book will remind and inspire you of all the great ways you are leading your team.

Please remember that your and your team's position will change depending on what's happening in your world, so it's important to keep taking stock.

Summary

- There is a gap between what research has uncovered that leads to greater wellbeing, engagement, resilience, and performance at work and what is being applied in organisations.
- Sales leaders who focus on on-field and off-field factors have teams that operate above the line.
- Sales leaders who don't emphasise the off-field are more likely to have teams sitting below the line.
- The focus as a start needs to be on sales leaders, given their massive influence on their team's success.

PART 2

CHAPTER THREE

BECOMING
STRONG

What are these strategies that promise such great outcomes? What deepens the engagement of workers? Which practices empower sales teams to achieve better results? What needs focus to thrive?

As mentioned earlier, the heavy lifting has been done for you. I've spent years scouring journals, reading books and articles, doing interviews, reviewing my own and others' experiences, and testing strategies out in real-world scenarios to find out what leads to deeper engagement, increased resilience, greater wellbeing and better performance in sales teams.

During this research, I uncovered six principles that create the foundation for you to become an outstanding sales leader as captured in Figure 2. The first letter of each principle, when combined, spells the word STRONG. I love a good acronym, and so do our brains, as it makes information so much easier to remember!

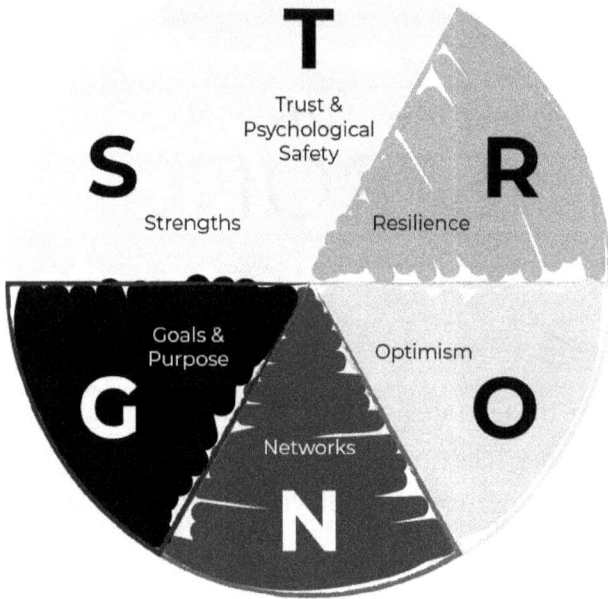

Figure 2: STRONG Model

The first principle focuses on *Strengths.* At their best, sales teams play to their strengths and manage their weaknesses so they're deeply engaged and satisfied with their work and experience lots of flow.[1, 2]

Next is *Trust and psychological safety,* which is about building trust between those around them and creating a safe environment where sales teams share and learn from one another. This strengthens their connections and makes them more resilient, creative and innovative, giving them an edge over their competitors.[3, 4, 5]

Given the number of setbacks and knockbacks sales teams regularly face, the third principle emphasises *Resilience* so sales teams can easily and effectively move forward and grow from struggles.[6]

Optimistic sales teams achieve more because they are positive about the future, they problem-solve, take action, and are more energetic, so the fourth principle is *Optimism.*[7, 8]

The fifth principle considers *Networks* and how the quality, not the quantity, of sales teams' relationships with all of those around them impact their energy and stress.[9, 10]

The sixth and final principle, *Goals and purpose,* centres on how sales teams can be intrinsically motivated and accountable to achieve their goals and more.[11, 12]

The good news is that these can be taught. Each principle encompasses great detail, which I'll unpack throughout the book. It's important to note that no single element is more important than the others. And each one alone will not lead to the outcomes you seek. But when they are all present within sales teams, they lay the foundations for thriving. Although based on research, you've probably realised that the STRONG principles aren't rocket science. When I've asked sales leaders about the characteristics of their top performers, they will list some of these. The same can be said for what leaders look for in potential new sales recruits. And intuitively, they make a lot of sense. But unfortunately, as mentioned earlier, sales leaders don't always focus on these principles. It's particularly disheartening, given that a number of sales teams operate below the line.

Off-field skills are the hardest to master.

There may be some reasons for this lack of implementation. (Or perhaps they are excuses.) Applying these principles can certainly take energy and time. Some leaders even brush them off as fluffy or soft because they're focused on the off-field element (the people) instead of the more technical aspects of selling. These leaders don't realise that off-field skills are the hardest to master.

Some of the principles may already align with how you lead your team. If so, this is good reinforcement and encouragement to keep doing what you're doing! Others may be new to you. Welcome any discomfort because such feelings are typically signs that you might be venturing outside your comfort zone into the growth arena. That's where you need to be!

The six STRONG principles are not exhaustive. Other factors, like personality types, will also lead your team to success, but this is a good start.

Please know I'm not suggesting you focus on all six principles at once. Rather, work out which you're doing well and keep them up. Then consider the one or two new principles you and your team need the most right now, and make them your focus.

A great way to work out how you're going with the STRONG principles is to rate yourself across each element using the following gauge.

How STRONG are you?

Let's see how well you are applying the STRONG principles with your team.

In the Agreement column, rate yourself across each element from 1 (Strongly disagree), 2 (Disagree), 3 (Neither agree nor disagree), 4 (Agree), to 5 (Strongly agree).

STRONG principle	Description	Agreement (1-5)
Strengths	I know the strengths of my team members and regularly look at ways to grow and develop them, and manage their weaknesses	
Trust and Psychological Safety	I have built a team that trusts each other, with a culture where team members can make mistakes, provide feedback, and share and learn from one another	
Resilience	I ensure that my team has the skills to cope well with challenges and grow from struggles, setbacks or change	
Optimism	I help my team develop an optimistic mindset so they are action-oriented, problem-solvers, energetic and positive	
Networks	I support my team in building high-quality connections with one another, our clients and stakeholders	
Goals and Purpose	I meet the needs of my team so they are intrinsically motivated to achieve our goals and purpose.	

- Where did you score the highest?
- Where did you score low?
- Which STRONG principles are a feature of your leadership?
- Which one or two elements will you prioritise (not necessarily where you scored the lowest) to help your team achieve better results?
- Which factors do your team need you to focus on?

This exercise demonstrates that you recognise which STRONG areas you already do well. Come back to this regularly to review your progress and decide on your next focus.

The following chapters explore each element of STRONG in greater detail. We'll examine why each is important for sales teams and how you, as the leader, can boost it.

CHAPTER FOUR

PLAYING TO STRENGTHS

To inspire people, don't show them your
superpowers; show them theirs.

— Alexander Den Heijer

As a leader of leaders in her real estate firm's property management division, Jane grappled with a growing issue. Some team members were reluctant to complete certain tasks. One example was Nick, an associate known for his exceptional client management skills but notorious for neglecting the monthly reporting essential for tracking sales, referrals and prospects. While Nick excelled in nurturing client relationships, he lacked enthusiasm for anything related to data. Jane was increasingly frustrated by his carelessness.

Jane repeatedly emphasised that reporting was a crucial part of the job. In her attempts to help Nick, she walked him through complex formulas, V-lookups and pivot tables. But the errors in his reports kept accumulating, leading Jane to question Nick's suitability for the role. However, Jane didn't consider that his avoidance might be because the task drained him rather than showed a lack of capability.

Every month, Jane met with Nick to meticulously dissect his Excel report, highlighting every mistake he had made. She treated Nick as though he were incompetent, which did little to nurture his engagement or motivation. Jane couldn't understand why there was no improvement and why Nick's energy and enthusiasm waned. Over time, the tension between Jane and Nick put a strain on their relationship, causing Nick's confidence to plummet. He dreaded the monthly report deadlines, and his morale was at an all-time low.

As part of a professional development day, the team participated in a strengths training session. During this workshop, Nick had an epiphany. He discovered that 'attention to detail' was one of his weaknesses. He wasn't good at it. And it depleted his energy. Everything started to make sense. But the session also revealed a whole lot of untapped potential within himself. Nick possessed a list of strengths that he excelled at and found energising that he had neglected.

Nick discovered that 'attention to detail' was one of his colleague Evan's top strengths, which prompted Nick to approach Evan about taking over his monthly reporting. It was as if Nick had given Evan a precious gift! Evan didn't see the additional responsibility as a burden but rather as an exciting opportunity to excel (pardon the pun) and contribute.

Jane was thrilled to receive an impeccably crafted report in her inbox each month, a far cry from the earlier frustrations with Nick's submissions. Meanwhile, Nick could focus on his other responsibilities and take on more tasks aligned with his strengths. As a result of the insights gained from the training session, Jane also focused on becoming better at tailoring the roles of her team members and reshuffling responsibilities to ensure that each team member played to their strengths.

Do we play to strengths?

We've all heard the saying to 'play to your strengths'. But as humans, we tend to focus on what's wrong, what's bad or what's weak about us, others, or a situation rather than what's right, what's great or what's strong. We are cruel creatures, aren't we? But it's not necessarily our fault.

The first challenge when trying to play to our strengths relates to something we are all born with. It's called negativity bias and is the in-built survival mechanism inherited from our ancestors, who needed it to survive. As they left their caves, they were constantly on the lookout for threats. This bias attuned them to danger, making them more likely to live. Fast forward to today, and while there aren't as many life-threatening predators around, the negativity bias means we focus on what we don't have, what's bad or what's wrong.

> Negativity bias encourages us to focus on our weaknesses and our shortcomings instead of our strengths.

What's more, the negativity bias encourages us to focus on our weaknesses and our shortcomings instead of our strengths. We do the same to the people around us, including our team members.

Think about it. How much more comfortable are you at listing all the things you're bad at instead of everything you excel at? Unless you have narcissistic tendencies, I'm sure you will say it's much easier to highlight all your weaknesses than your strengths.

While we're hard-wired to focus on the negative, we've become fixated on trying to fill our gaps to be well-rounded and good at everything. Yet this approach doesn't energise us or have us performing at our best. The opposite occurs. Trying to fix our weaknesses or even turn them into a strength leaves us drained and demotivated – hardly a recipe for success! Remember, it takes something like 10,000 hours to turn a weakness into a strength – I can think of much better things to do with that time.

Athletes don't try their luck at sports they're weak in. They focus on what they're great at to increase their chances of winning. If they're a good tennis player, they play tennis. If they can swim really well, they concentrate on being a swimmer.

The second issue is that workplaces also have an in-built negativity bias. As a result, they tend to influence workers and leaders to focus on filling gaps, fixing problems, and turning weaknesses into strengths – just as Jane was doing with her team.

Performance or development conversations tend to be structured around what someone needs to improve rather than what they're doing well and how this can be built upon.

It's the same when we give feedback throughout the year; we focus more on the constructive rather than the positive. We often don't ask our clients about what we're doing well but rather we encourage them to tell us what we could do better. And when we build strategies or team plans (SWOT analysis anyone?), we tend to consider where we're failing and how to fix that, rather than giving up on that idea and focusing on improving the areas we're good at so they become great!

And finally, in Australia in particular, the tall poppy syndrome seems to stop us from talking about our strengths and what we're great at. Why? Because we don't want to be seen to brag, for fear that we might be resented, disliked or criticised by our peers.

> # The target ratio is 80% focus on strengths and 20% on weaknesses.

These challenges get in the way of playing to our strengths and cause us to focus more on our weaknesses. In practice, most workplaces spend about 80% of their time and efforts on what needs fixing, what their gaps and weaknesses are, and only about 20% on what's working well, their strengths and what's right about them.[1]

Playing to strengths isn't about ignoring weaknesses but managing them and flipping the 80/20 rule. If there's currently an 80% focus on weaknesses and 20% on strengths, swap these around. The target ratio is 80% focus on strengths and 20% on weaknesses.

What are strengths?

Alex Linley, a world-leading researcher on the subject, describes a strength as 'a pre-existing capacity for a particular way of behaving, thinking or feeling that is authentic and energising to the user, and enables optimal functioning, development and performance'.[2]

This is my favourite definition because it highlights why they differ from weaknesses (particularly the energy element), because we can all think of things that we're good at but find draining or hate doing. Hardly a recipe for high performance!

Strengths should light us up rather than deplete us. It's probably something we've practised over time, so the neural pathway is well-developed.[3] We feel confident using our strengths. Sometimes, we're unaware of them because they come so naturally. They're just how we are and what we do.

You may wonder if strength is simply another word for talent and capability. And the answer is no. Although there are some overlapping characteristics between the three, don't be confused. A *talent* is a specific aptitude or skill someone has a natural affinity for. A *capability* is someone's capacity to perform a certain task that might require skill and has been developed over time through learning or training. And a *strength* is something that someone performs well; it energises them, and they enjoy it.

In this chapter, we'll talk about using strengths, which have been shown to boost engagement, wellbeing, resilience and performance at work.[4, 5, 6]

Strengths should light us up rather than deplete us.

Yet despite these incredible known outcomes, only one-third of people know their strengths and even fewer use them in their roles.[7] And very few workplaces can say that they have a strengths-based culture. That means many people are unaware and have not unlocked some of the great potential within them.

Why strengths?

The Greek philosopher Aristotle was the first to suggest that for people to be the best they could be, they needed to live according to their strengths. Playing to strengths comes with many impressive outcomes uncovered in research over recent decades, particularly the last twenty years. The field of positive psychology has given a new renaissance to strengths research, with new theories, assessments and interventions, so now we know a lot more about the benefits of strengths, particularly at work.

> Strengths are our brain's way of performing at its best.

Strengths are our brain's way of performing at its best. And if that's happening, it must also have a positive impact elsewhere. Research has shown that workers who know their strengths are more engaged and perform better. They use their internal resources to overcome hurdles and have greater wellbeing.[8] Using strengths provides the best opportunities for growth and success because we're more confident and, therefore, more likely to achieve our goals when using strengths.[9]

Focusing on weaknesses only ever leads to average performance. We will never outperform the average if we focus on our weaknesses. But that doesn't mean they aren't important. Paying attention to our gaps or shortcomings is a way to prevent failure. When we build on what's working well, we can exceed average performance.[10] That's a much smarter strategy for business success.

> Strengths really are a superpower.

Strengths use has also been connected to greater energy, confidence, goal attainment, happiness, less stress, satisfaction, growth and development, creativity, and agility. When leaders uncover team members' strengths, they acquire new skills and capabilities without adding new workers. It's a concept known as 'quiet hiring'.

Strengths really are a superpower.

How does a leader play to strengths?

As a sales leader, you are more self-aware when you understand your strengths. You know which areas you do well and what should be your focus for future development. The beauty of being a leader is that you can manage your weaknesses through delegation and by surrounding yourself with a team whose strengths counterbalance your weaknesses. Knowing your strengths will also give you confidence to navigate current and future complex working environments.[11]

Knowing the strengths of your team members helps you understand them better. Your team members are typically equipped with an aptitude for sales and follow a sales process. But they also each bring a unique set of strengths. For example, they might excel at telling stories, diving into detail, analysing data, or making connections between people. They may love learning and enjoy exploring other products and services, so you are on top of your competitors' offers. Or they might be a great counterpoint, bringing in a different viewpoint to others.

When you know your team members' strengths, you can align them with appropriate responsibilities and tasks. This process is called 'job crafting', which is covered in more detail at the end of this chapter. This results in a team that is energised in performing their tasks.

If your team members' strengths are unknown or don't get much play, they lie dormant. The risk is that when a situation calls for these particular strengths, the task might not fall to the right person. These are missed opportunities for empowerment.

Just as you build your leadership awareness when you know your strengths, the same occurs when team members realise theirs and reveal them to each other. Awareness is a pathway to building trust, which is fundamental for a thriving team. (More on trust in the next chapter.) Teams are more collaborative and productive when they play to their strengths.

Drawing out your team's strengths supports a diversity and inclusion focus by encouraging people to own their individuality. Rather than fitting everyone into boxes, playing to strengths encourages teams to bring their best, most authentic selves to work.

In Part One, I cautioned that declining engagement is one of the greatest global challenges facing sales leaders. A recent Gallup study shows that engagement in Australian workplaces is only 20%.[12] We know that a large part of engagement is attributable to the leader. This is a major issue when employee engagement is a significant driver of job satisfaction and organisational commitment, as the fallout from this trend is costly. Yet when leaders know and play to their sales team's strengths, they increase engagement and improve performance.[13]

Workplace burnout is also on the rise. One reason is that we lack the resources to meet our demands.[14] Strengths are an internal resource. If we can't provide more time, people, or money, we should encourage teams to use their strengths to meet challenges and achieve goals.

Strengths-based sales teams have an advantage.

A strength is something you're good at, do often, and that energises you. This knowledge can prevent leaders from falling into the trap of appointing someone who might be good at the job but isn't energised or motivated. You can also use this definition to identify people's strengths more accurately and consistently and to craft roles that tap into their skills, energy and motivation.

Strengths-based sales teams have an advantage. Their leaders support them to use their strengths to cope with challenges and stress and achieve their goals. When managers adopt a strengths-based approach, they can personalise work. As a result, these teams stand out as they typically outperform their competitors.

How do you play to strengths?

Playing to strengths is one of the easiest and most effective ways to boost the engagement of teams. But more than that, when leaders leverage the superpowers of themselves and their team members, they can also increase resilience, wellbeing and performance.

When we know the strengths of our team, we can build deeper connection and trust (see Chapter Five on Trust). Leaders can also ensure that they set their teams up so they're all at their best. And manage their own weaknesses by having people on their team that fill their gaps. It's a smart strategy that makes leaders look good.

Now that I've sold you on the power of strengths, what can you try with your team?

Identify strengths

You need to identify strengths before you can play to them.

Several survey questionnaires can help, including Values in Action (VIA), CliftonStrengths and Strengths Profile. CliftonStrengths provides reports specifically for people in sales. Although this formal approach takes time, it's a great first step and can build your language around strengths.

As you understand what strengths look like and how they show up, you will start to spot them in your team members.

For example, look for people doing work that lights them up or notice them in flow. These are great opportunities to recognise and celebrate your team members.

Find flow

Once strengths are identified, the next step is to use them more.

Psychologist Mihaly Csikszentmihalyi identified the concept of flow as when you are fully absorbed in a task.[15] It's that feeling of being 'in the zone'. You are performing at your best, but it feels effortless because you are using your strengths.

Given how much time we spend at work, we want it to be a place where flow occurs. Flow is a great way to engage and motivate your people, particularly when times are tough, as it energises them, they feel a sense of accomplishment, and it boosts their positivity and reduces stress.

Flow is different for each of us. It might be meaningful conversations with a client for one person or reviewing sales pipelines for another.

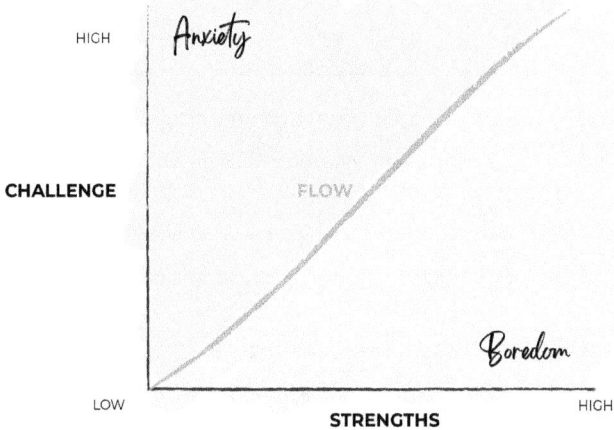

Figure 3: Flow diagram (adapted from Csikszentmihalyi, 2008)

As Figure 3 shows, we get bored if tasks aren't challenging enough. Conversely, if the tasks are too challenging, and we don't feel we have the strengths to succeed, we become stressed and anxious.

Consider where your team members are on the map. Are they in the flow zone? Do you need to ramp up or down their challenges? Or perhaps dial up or down their use of strengths? Do you need to remove obstacles that might be in the way of flow?

We want teams to experience flow as much as possible, as this is when they are most engaged and performing at their best.

Job crafting

Job crafting is the physical and cognitive changes made in the tasks and responsibilities of a role to align with a team member's strengths.[16] It can be when you proactively craft the number, scope, or types of tasks your team members perform.

When done well, job crafting is like a tailored suit (rather than off the peg), where your job fits you perfectly.

To start this process, ask team members to note all their tasks and responsibilities and divide them into those they enjoy doing (where their strengths lie) and those that drain them.

Consider how you might give them more activities they enjoy doing. How could draining tasks be modified? Could they be assigned to someone else who would enjoy them? Or could they use one of their strengths to make the task more energising? (Remember Nick at the start of this chapter?) Or could they simply think differently about the task?

Summary

- Strengths are things we are good at, enjoy doing and that energise us.
- Decades of research have shown that using our strengths increases engagement, wellbeing, resilience and performance at work.
- Negativity bias, our workplaces and tall poppy syndrome encourage us to focus on our weaknesses and gaps.
- Truly playing to strengths takes a mindset shift and lots of practice.

CHAPTER FIVE

BUILDING TRUST AND PSYCHOLOGICAL SAFETY

No passion effectively robs the mind of all its powers of acting and reasoning as fear.

— Edmund Burke

Simon, a dedicated sales leader in the competitive technology industry, faced a challenge affecting his high-performing team's success. His team was responsible for selling cutting-edge software solutions to businesses, and the pressure to meet ambitious KPIs set by the organisation's executive team was relentless.

The team should have been a force to be reckoned with, as it comprised many talented individuals who had consistently hit their targets. However, a troubling issue had emerged. Instead of collaborating harmoniously to achieve their goals, team members felt locked in fierce competition, driven by the immense pressure they were under.

Their once-vibrant weekly meetings had transformed into tense gatherings. The easy banter that had fostered their friendships was missing, replaced by limited and strictly work-related communication. In the past, the team had shared everything – including their triumphs and setbacks. Lately, though, Simon sensed that some team members were holding back and concealing valuable information about their progress.

Gone were the days when they would rally together during tough times, supporting each other through thick and thin. Now, the team was reticent, hesitant to offer suggestions, share ideas, or discuss ways to overcome the challenges they faced. Simon couldn't help but feel the growing rift among his once-tight-knit team. Something had gone off.

After one particularly sombre meeting, Simon decided to address the issue head-on. He pulled aside Lisa, one of the team members he had a good rapport with, and candidly inquired about the silence and lack of collaboration. Lisa opened up, revealing that the team had begun to feel that any contributions would be met with criticism, judgement, or even mockery. This pattern had increasingly emerged in recent meetings.

As Simon listened to Lisa, the gravity of the situation became clear. Trust was absent among his team members, and psychological safety was virtually non-existent within *their culture. The external pressures of ambitious KPIs and the team's internal dynamics were eroding their morale and productivity.*

Recognising the urgency of the situation, Simon knew that restoring trust and fostering psychological safety would have to be his top priority. He understood that without these crucial elements, his team would continue to falter, unable to harness their full potential.

What is trust?

Our relationships with those we work with play a fundamental role in our performance. What's more, those connections greatly impact how engaged we are in our work and lives, our resilience and our health. That's why there's a whole chapter later focused on the importance of our networks.

But there's more to relationships than we might think. The trust and psychological safety created by relationships are essential for us to thrive.

Trust has long been regarded as a prerequisite for *all* relationships. It typically exists between individuals and is about having each other's back. It's when we are confident in the reliability, integrity and intention of another. Trust is created when we can confidently predict and believe others will act in certain ways and keep their commitments. Trust is hard to build and easily lost by not keeping your word.

In sales, we have to trust our colleagues. We must be sure that our work buddies won't overstep their boundaries and will stay within their patch. They won't approach our clients or speak badly of us in front of others – including our prospects.

> Trust doesn't come from words; it's about action.

Trust is evident within teams when people confide, support, share and learn from each other. Without trust, the opposite occurs. You have a team full of *hunters*, potentially competing against one another, leading to an unhealthy atmosphere of rivalry. Without trust, team members tend to keep information to themselves for their personal advantage. They don't care when their colleagues are struggling. Rather than working together, their focus is on outdoing that person. A lack of trust is also what causes accountability to wallow. Such a negative environment decreases team cohesion, hinders growth and compromises the team's overall results.

Leaders must trust their team members and manage them according to the outcomes achieved. When trust is absent, there is dysfunction. Most leaders will say they trust their team members to do their jobs, but trust doesn't come from words; it's about action.

We question how much leaders really trust their team when they resort to micro-managing, wanting to know the details of every minute of their day. These actions can lead to a cycle of distrust, where team members feel their abilities, actions and choices are constantly analysed and often doubted.

Why do we need trust?

Undoubtedly, one of the first things you are told when foraying into the world of sales is the importance of building trust with your customers. Trust makes selling *easier*. When your customers trust you, they're more likely to share their needs, concerns or pain points and consider your recommendations. You have greater influence over

Trust drives sales success.

a client's decision when they trust you. And they tend to be more loyal to you. Over the long term, trust drives sales success, contributing to your organisation's overall growth and reputation.

What about trust with your colleagues?

Building trust with your colleagues is equally important but rarely stressed enough. Trust between leaders and teams, and within teams, is vital to thrive.

We collaborate and communicate better when we trust our peers. We're more likely to share ideas, insights and best practices, leading to improved decision-making and problem-solving. When we share what we know, we create opportunities to learn and grow from one another.

Trusting teams are more likely to align their actions and work together to achieve common goals. They support and help one another to overcome challenges. Even though there may be conflict, trust simplifies resolutions as team members are more willing to engage in open discussion to address the issues.

When trust is present, the atmosphere within the team is far more positive and continues to grow, amplifying people's satisfaction with their work. They achieve more together than is possible alone as the group has greater synergies.

If the leader is trusted, adverse reactions from employees can be limited when difficult decisions need to be made.[1]

What's more, when we think about the best person for the job, we shouldn't necessarily choose the highest performer. American author Simon Sinek challenges us to think about how trustworthy they are, as this relates to their character, whereas their performance relates to their competence.[2] Sinek argues that character is a far better indicator of a quality employee who will positively contribute to your team over the longer term.

Can a team perform to a high level *and* lack trust? Yes. But while that might work in the short term, such performance won't be sustainable over time. Without trust, there's a lack of collaboration, missed opportunities and more conflict and tension. All of which reduce performance in an unhealthy, unproductive working environment.

Trust really is the glue that holds sales teams together.

There's a big difference between teams with internal trust and teams that happen to work together. Trust really is the glue that holds sales teams together.

What is psychological safety?

Psychological safety is often confused with trust, and while they share similarities, they are entirely different concepts.

Trust is the belief one person has about the other, so it involves the interactions between them and exists in the mind.

Psychological safety refers to the environment where team members feel comfortable taking risks, expressing opinions, making mistakes and being themselves. Such an environment highlights that we are all human and perfectly imperfect. In this light, psychological safety is associated more with group norms, or how group members feel they can behave.

Leaders either build psychological safety or are obstacles to it. It either is or isn't part of your culture and the practices your team do because it's just business as usual. Leaders must create an environment where psychological safety can grow, including ensuring the team adopts the right mindsets and behaviours. And communicate and uphold what is and isn't acceptable within the team.

> Leaders either build psychological safety or are obstacles to it.

Unfortunately, most of us have been exposed to workplaces that lack psychological safety. In case you've forgotten, here's what they look like. We worry about the negative consequences of making mistakes, so we blame others. We withhold our opinions and stressors for fear of embarrassment or assertions of incompetence. We don't take risks because we're anxious about failure, and we don't expose our vulnerabilities or struggles for concern that we will look weak.

We don't speak up because we don't want to criticise something that our manager or peers have come up with. We don't have solid data to back up our claims, but we rely on our gut. We don't want to speak up if our manager's boss is present because we worry it will be a career-limiting move.

When targets aren't met, finger-pointing and blame are commonplace. Instead of the group analysing what went wrong and trying to find solutions, teams avoid accountability and deflect responsibility onto others to protect themselves from potential repercussions. All of which is disastrous in the long term.

It's a horrible place to be. You're constantly second-guessing, not backing yourself, hiding away, or pretending you're OK rather than seeking help. In this environment, problems are ignored or not uncovered, so they build up over time, making them much harder to address later.

Have you ever been in a sales forecasting meeting where budgets are set way too high and are virtually unachievable, but everyone agrees to them anyway? Or when your team members are running two different CRMs – one that's public for the whole team to see and one that's private for their eyes only so they don't reveal certain information? Or when your team members stop telling you how deals are going? These are all examples of where psychological safety isn't present.

Psychological safety exists when people are inclusive, share and value opinions, offer new ideas, ask questions, voice their concerns, own up to mistakes and learn from them without fear of judgement or ridicule.[3]

According to Drs Michelle McQuaid and Paige Williams from the Leaders Lab, psychological safety isn't just some cosy situation where people are close friends chasing rainbows and butterflies. It's where groups share in challenges and pressures, communicate honestly with one another, and work through ideas or problems together. They may even disagree, but it's healthy and productive conflict. [4]

In sales teams, psychological safety might also show up as team members role-playing part of the sales process so they can learn from one another. Information is shared about deals being worked on. Clients are referred across the team and there is openness to role shadowing – particularly for someone new.

Why do we need psychological safety?

Decades of research have found that psychological safety significantly contributes to team success.[5] Need I say more?

Although it's a relatively new concept, psychological safety delivers many great outcomes to sales teams. Hence, the rising interest over recent years, particularly since Project Aristotle, a longitudinal study at Google, sought to find out what made the best teams. The researchers wanted to understand whether demographics, skills, education and gender were factors. They didn't find anything, so they looked at team norms, routines and rituals and discovered that higher-performing teams shared one thing: psychological safety.[6]

Psychological safety has shifted traditional thinking about exposing our vulnerabilities, struggles and mistakes at work. Rather than hiding away, psychological safety suggests we should be rewarded for this sharing. That's because by doing so, we feel safe to come up with new ways of doing things, take risks, bring in diverse ideas and ask for help. All of which encourages a learning culture so we achieve better outcomes in the long term.

Higher-performing teams shared one thing: psychological safety.

This is especially important when solving complex problems or facing huge challenges, as it makes us feel safe to navigate these ups and downs and can help us overcome these hurdles more easily. It also creates space to reflect with our peers when deals haven't gone as well as they could so we can learn from these and improve going forward.

Psychological safety allows us to be more creative and innovative, which can be a competitive advantage in most (if not all) industries. Psychological safety doesn't mean we don't fail, but we regard failure as an opportunity for learning and innovation. We reduce workarounds and shortcuts that create problems in the long term.

Leaders who are more vulnerable forge stronger connections with their team members. Teams work better in a psychologically safe environment and are more engaged in their roles.[7] They experience a sense of belonging, so they are more committed to their teams, and trust and respect are enhanced. As team members feel more valued and respected, they're more motivated to take ownership of their responsibilities and goals, further contributing to team success. Psychological safety reduces stress as the team isn't worried about negative consequences.

> If we're not seeking their ideas, we're leaving possibilities and potential untapped.

Like trust, a sales team may still meet their KPIs in the short term when psychological safety is absent. Yet, over the long term, negative consequences will impact the team's success. We might have highly knowledgeable and talented individuals, but if we're not seeking their ideas, we're leaving possibilities and potential untapped. Imagine what we might discover, create, or achieve when that is unleashed.

If both trust and psychological safety are missing from sales teams, you'll have a group of lone hunters focused on themselves and their targets at the expense of team success. This can lead to a toxic culture as the lack of collaboration or team cohesiveness has a huge toll on wellbeing. When people are in this constant state of stress, they fear failure and feel even more pressure to perform, which can result in burnout. Over time, team members become disillusioned by the toxic culture and look for jobs elsewhere.

When team members trust one another, they collaborate well and feel more psychologically safe. The team's culture thrives. People feel they belong and are respected, supported and encouraged. You're less likely to lose your star performers and others will want to join your team.

How do we achieve trust and psychological safety?

Trust and psychological safety are created over time through consistent actions between individuals, leaders and their teams.

Building this environment starts with you as the leader. You set the tone of the culture and should be the example of the behaviours you wish to see in your team. It's your job to create an environment where people feel safe and trust one another. That might mean exposing your vulnerabilities, sharing your failures or stepping outside your comfort zone. It can also be about ensuring everyone has a voice, can provide input, and contribute ideas.

As discussed in Chapter Four, trust can be fostered by knowing more about another person, including their strengths.

So, what could you try?

Delegate responsibility

Giving away control is one of the best ways to tell your team you trust them. You convey trust when you set clear goals for your team and leave them to work out how to get the job done. Delegating says you trust they have the skills to carry out the task. That's especially so when you give away responsibilities that make you look good or impact your success.

Seek input

Build psychological safety by ensuring everyone on your team has a voice and that their opinions matter. Actively invite engagement during team meetings and other forums by being curious, asking great questions and rewarding opinions, suggestions and new ideas. Your team will continue to do this if they know they are being heard, their comments are valued and you respond respectfully and with appreciation.

If you're unsure about levels of trust and psychological safety, give your teams different options for providing feedback. These might be via anonymous surveys, one-on-ones, with their peers, or chats with other teams in your workplace.

Create a learning culture

Make your team environment one where everyone is continuously learning. And that includes you. Allow permission to fail when testing new ways of doing things, making changes to products or services, or looking at different or new clients or markets.

In a learning culture, failures are seen as opportunities to grow and develop. To destigmatise failure, share your own struggles and shortcomings or acknowledge your weaknesses, be vulnerable, acknowledge when something is a weakness or when you don't know something, or ask for help. A great way to build a learning culture is by regularly using The Learning Loop in meetings and conversations, and following wins and losses with clients.[8] This framework reinforces strengths and normalises struggle, making it a regular part of any process. It also encourages us to see those setbacks as learnings and to inform future efforts.

The Learning Loop model in Figure 4, asks us to consider: 1. Act – what is it that you tried? 2. Assess – what went well, where did you struggle, what did you learn? 3. Adjust – what will you try next?

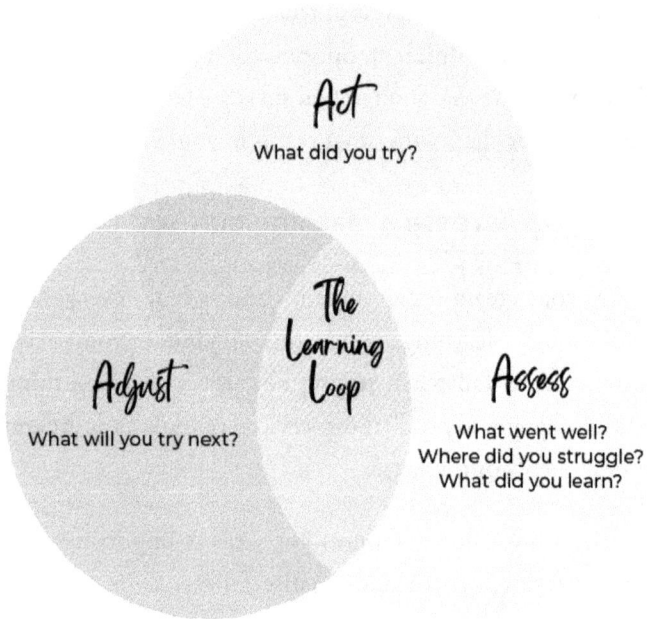

Act
What did you try?

The Learning Loop

Adjust
What will you try next?

Assess
What went well?
Where did you struggle?
What did you learn?

Figure 4: The Learning Loop (adapted from McQuaid & Melville, 2019)

Summary

- Trust and psychological safety are foundational relationship elements contributing to sales team success.
- Although they appear similar, trust exists between individuals and psychological safety is embedded within the culture of a team or organisation.
- Trust and psychological safety encourage collaboration, innovation, creativity, resilience and risk-taking. All of which give a sales team a competitive edge.
- Trust and psychological safety are hard to build and easily destroyed.

CHAPTER SIX

STRENGTHENING RESILIENCE

Don't judge me by my success; judge me by how many times I fell down and got back up again.

— Nelson Mandela

Georgia leads a sales team within a telecommunications company that faces the difficult challenge of achieving new client targets with less-than-ideal products. Like anyone in sales, the team had previously encountered their fair share of setbacks and rejections. However, Georgia noticed a crucial difference among the team members when confronting these challenges.

Within her team, Georgia observed two distinct groups. On one hand, after working their way through their call list without securing a sale, there were those who would find their motivation and enthusiasm depleted by the twentieth call of the day. Instead of channelling their energy into strategising on improving and increasing their chances of success on the next call, they tended to dwell on their failures. They began assigning blame to external factors, such as the perceived quality of their product, and doubting their abilities, leading to thoughts like, 'I'm no good at this'.

In contrast, Georgia also noticed another group within her team, exemplified by individuals like Emma. These team members also worked through their call lists without achieving a sale. However, when they reached the twentieth call, despite repeated failures on the previous nineteen calls, they picked up the phone with an unwavering belief that a sale would be made on the upcoming call. They persevered, driven by the conviction that if the current call didn't succeed, the next one, or the one after that, would. They embraced each setback as an opportunity for growth, a chance to review their approach, seek advice from their peers and learn from the experience.

Remarkably, this second group never viewed setbacks as defeats but as integral parts of their journey. Each challenge only fuelled their determination to improve and succeed. Consequently, those like Emma consistently outperformed their peers and achieved higher levels of success.

The first group's motivation and morale gradually eroded over time, leading to subpar performance. The ripple effect of their lack of drive was even more concerning, as it permeated parts of the team and fostered a toxic atmosphere in those areas.

In every team, there are those who, when confronted with challenges, tend to wallow and let adversity weigh them down, while others rise to the occasion and carry on with determination. The key distinction between these two types of salespeople isn't their hunger for success. It's their resilience – the ability to bounce back from setbacks, maintain an unwavering belief in their abilities, and persist in the face of adversity.

Georgia realised resilience was the critical factor that set apart salespeople like Emma, who persevered after the twentieth setback from those who hesitated to pick up the phone again. Resilience was the ingredient that fueled their enduring determination and ultimately led them to achieve more.

What is resilience?

The key role of a salesperson is to sell. You and I both know that isn't easy. Even the best salespeople can find selling hard. It's particularly so in today's challenging market conditions; clients' expectations are increasing, and products and services are getting harder to differentiate. Because of that, many salespeople are unsure whether they will be able to achieve their KPIs. Nevertheless, they persist with their prospecting. Well, some do. And some don't, as the story above illustrates. The difference between the two is not down to their selling skills, but resilience, which leads to one group being more successful than the other.

Resilience is a term that gets thrown around a lot these days. Often, it's referred to as bouncing back, being buoyant or recovering quickly from challenges. Yet I like the definition offered by two of the world's leading researchers in resilience, who suggest that resilience is 'a pattern of positive adaptation in the face of significant risk or adversity'.[1]

I like this definition because it speaks to positive actions rather than the harmful activities we might turn to, such as drinking, gambling or excessive shopping. It's also about taking control over what we can in those circumstances. 'This has happened, now what can I do?' It's about staying on course and persisting when times are tough. It's picking up the phone again even when you've been knocked back time and time again.

To be resilient, we might have to flex in some way – perhaps in how we think ('this challenge is a learning opportunity'), how we act ('I need to seek some support here') or how we feel ('I need to stay calm'). And because of that flex, we're more likely to overcome the challenge positively, which can build other resources to draw upon when we come up against our next challenge.

In this light, we can take the concept of resilience one step further. Lucy Hone, another global authority on resilience, speaks to the idea of post-traumatic growth.[2] As we rebuild following difficult events, we might find ourselves doing things differently, grow in some way or change direction because of the adversity.

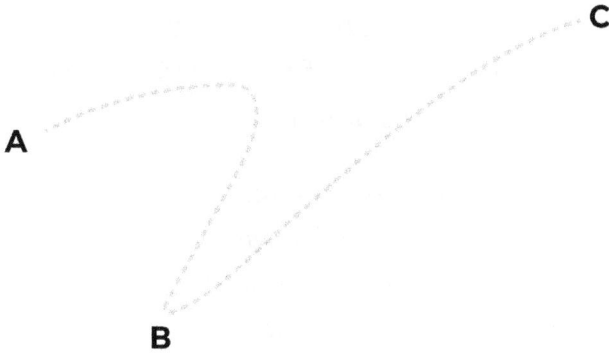

C

A

B

Figure 5: Growing from struggle (adapted from Hone, 2017)

Resilience isn't just about bouncing back to where we were before the challenge, as illustrated in Figure 5. Instead, because of the growth or new skills we have developed, we might find that we are stronger, better equipped and more able to overcome future hurdles. Instead of returning to point A, we find ourselves at point C.

Consider the pandemic; we all weathered the same storm in different boats. Those boats represent what we had in our resilience toolbox – the strategies to cope with our situation. Were you in a battleship with loads of crew, life rafts and navigation technology? Or were you in an inflatable dinghy with no lifejacket, lights or oars? The contents of your resilience toolbox dictated the boat you were in and how well you got through the COVID-19 storm.

As we emerged from that difficult period, most of us could say we developed a new skill or knowledge, a new way of doing things, or even a new way of living because of what we endured – even if it was the ability to use Zoom to engage with our clients. Because of that experience, we're better prepared for the next storm. This is post-traumatic growth.

Aside from the individual resilience needed in sales, we must also consider the collective resilience of our teams. Individual resilience is like learning to swim, but collective resilience is building a boat for all. Support from other people helps us get through tough times. The human race couldn't have made it this far alone. Sales teams are resilient when they care for and back each other and function well together in the face of common challenges.

Resilient sales teams learn from one another so they will develop the behaviours or norms of what's needed to get through. They provide emotional support and encouragement, which helps individuals cope with stress and remain optimistic. Collective resilience encourages better teamwork, higher morale and, therefore, greater performance.

Resilient individuals build collective resilience.

Resilient individuals build collective resilience.

Why do we need resilience in sales?

In conversations with salespeople, many have suggested that you must be hungry to be good at sales. You've got to really want the sale and do whatever it takes to get it.

While that is true to some extent, resilience is more important than hunger.

On any given day, salespeople face many different challenges. Markets fluctuate, inflation rises, clients change their minds, negative feedback is received, or competitors launch a better, less expensive product.

Rejection is a normal part of sales (more so than other roles). Salespeople know they won't win every time, even though they will try to. Knockbacks are expected, but that doesn't mean they don't hurt. It's true, even when the rejection isn't a reflection of the salesperson but due to factors outside their control.

Given the high failure rates, a salesperson's ability to recover from setbacks is critical. You probably know people who haven't been able to succeed in sales, most likely because they didn't have the resilience to persist and sustain their motivation.

As in the story at the start of this chapter, some salespeople believe 'the next call will be the one where I will make the sale', so they act differently. They pick up the phone and make the twentieth call, and because they persevere, they're typically more successful in the long run. Compare that with their colleague who thinks 'the next call will be another rejection', so they don't make the call. Salespeople need to learn how to handle rejection positively, view it as an opportunity to learn and grow, and keep persisting to find other customers to close deals with. Those attributes equate to resilience. Without it, you might find you have a salesperson who ruminates, procrastinates, avoids challenges, is demotivated or withdrawn. Hardly a recipe for a thriving team member.

Aside from its ability to help us cope well with challenges, resilience can also support us in reducing the impact of stress and exhaustion – exactly what many of us need right now. Mental and physical exhaustion are key characteristics of burnout.[3] And given burnout has been linked to thoughts of quitting, you could say that resilience reduces turnover. People are less stressed when they're resilient, so they tend to be more satisfied with their jobs. When job satisfaction is higher, they are more engaged and perform better in their roles.

> It takes resilience to thrive, not just survive, in sales.

Resilience is the base element we need to get us operating above the line and closer towards thriving.

It takes resilience to thrive, not just survive, in sales.

How do we become more resilient?

Given the increasing complexity of our lives, it's no longer enough to rely on existing coping skills, especially in sales roles. The good news is that we can build resilience, even though it's rarely taught as a skill for sales teams.

Resilience research has uncovered several strategies that can be used to increase our ability to bounce forward from challenges. We've covered some in earlier chapters. Self-awareness and using strengths can boost resilience (see Chapter Four on Strengths). Adopting an optimistic mindset puts us in the best headspace (see Chapter Seven on Optimism). Strong connections support you in times of need (see Chapter Eight on Networks). Understanding your purpose can help you stay on course (see Chapter Nine on Goals and Purpose). Team resilience comes from an environment of trust and psychological safety (see Chapter Five) and a shared sense of purpose (see Chapter Nine on Goals and Purpose).

And there's more you can do to boost the resilience of your team.

So, what can you try?

Focus on what you can control

Our minds wander. A 2010 Harvard study estimates that almost half the time we're doing one thing, we're actually thinking about something else.[4] So perhaps our attention is our scarcest resource, not time or money. It's no surprise we're struggling to focus, given the 24-hour news cycle, the barrage of social media and the countless distractions. The real reason we lose focus most often is because we are looking to escape some kind of discomfort, such as stress, anxiety, loneliness or boredom. But given focus is so valuable, we need to improve our skills with practice.

The psychologist Julian Rotter developed the concept of the locus of control in the 1950s.[5] Stephen Covey extended and popularised the idea in his book *The 7 Habits of Highly Effective People*.[6] Rotter suggested we should focus on things within our control (the inner circle), which maintain wellbeing, energy and productivity. These often relate to our thoughts, emotions and actions. Even though we are concerned by them, there's no point focusing on the things we can't control (in the outer circle) because they add to stress and waste time and energy. Figure 6 illustrates these circles.

When your team faces a challenge, encourage them to focus on what they can control in that moment. What's the smallest action they could take? How could they see things differently? What would make them feel better? In sales, we might not be able to control our prospect's intention to buy, the competitor's product or changing interest rates, but there are many factors we do control, including making calls, seeking referrals and building strong relationships.

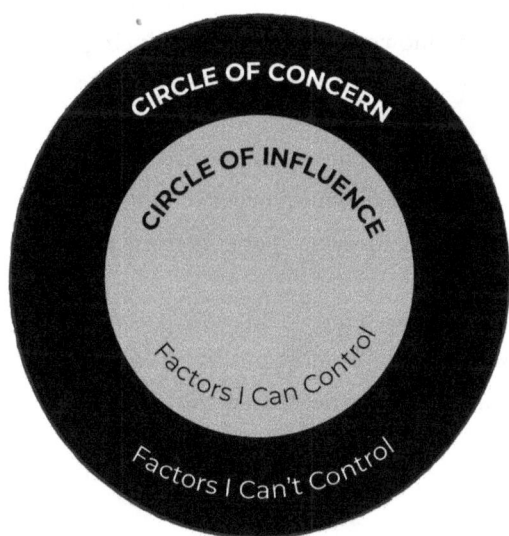

Figure 6: Circles of influence and concern (adapted from Covey, 2020; Rotter, 1966)

Boost positive emotions

When we experience position emotions like joy, love, interest and excitement, we become more resilient. Say what? A leading researcher on emotions, Barbara Fredrickson, found that when we experience positivity in the present, our minds are broadened. We become more creative, flexible, innovative and better able to problem-solve.[7]

We also strengthen our connections with those around us when we're in a positive state. We build social support and skills like problem-solving, so when we next encounter a challenge, we draw on these resources to overcome it. Research has shown that teams experiencing more positive than negative emotions perform better.[8]

It's more than just feeling good; positive emotions positively impact workplaces, while negative emotions often lead to burnout, absenteeism, poor performance and higher turnover.[9]

Asking your team to be more positive is easier said than done. We are surrounded by negativity, and because of our human bias towards negativity, we tend to pay more attention to the bad than the good.

As a leader, you can boost the positivity in your team by encouraging them to be grateful, use humour or show kindness. Start team meetings with a joke, undertake regular check-ins to see what's going well, celebrate achievements, recognise birthdays and regularly express appreciation for one another.

Emotions are contagious, so when the leader is in a positive state, the team is more likely to follow suit.[10]

Rest and recover

Resilience isn't about toughing it out or grinning and bearing it. It's not a matter of wearing yourself out as you work towards your targets. Research shows that rest and recovery are fundamental to resilience so problems don't multiply.[11] That doesn't just mean recharging over the weekend or on annual leave. Rest and recovery need to be incorporated into all our days. This might require a mindset shift for some people who believe recovery is a reward for working hard. Yet well-rested employees are resilient and, therefore, more able to perform at their best every day.

Try some of these activities to encourage your team to rest and recover:

- Practice mindfulness: This can include meditation, breathing activities, colouring books and even eating mindfully.

- Connect with others: Create opportunities for regular team catch-ups.

- Hobbies: Encourage your team to pursue interests outside work that allow their brains to rest.

- Exercise: Make time for your team to exercise during their lunch break, or before or after work.

- Holidays: Ensure your team takes regular breaks throughout the year.

Summary

- Knockbacks and setbacks are common in sales, so salespeople need to be resilient to cope well.
- Resilience can be the difference between salespeople who successfully achieve their goals and those who don't.
- Sales teams move from 'below the line' to 'above the line' by being resilient.
- Individual and collective resilience is needed in sales teams.

CHAPTER SEVEN

LEARNING OPTIMISM

A pessimist sees the difficulty in every opportunity, an optimist sees the opportunity in every difficulty.

— Winston Churchill

A global insurance company embarked on a massive annual recruitment drive for many years. The organisation invested millions of dollars in training to equip its sales recruits with the necessary skills. Despite this substantial investment, the company faced a big dilemma. They were losing a staggering 50% of their newly recruited people within their first year on the job. And by the end of the fourth year, close to 80% of their sales force had abandoned ship. Clearly, their return on investment for their training initiatives was far from optimal!

Recognising the urgent need for change, Peter, the sales GM, understood they couldn't continue down this path. Seeking a solution, he turned to the expertise of a clinical psychologist renowned for his work on optimism and its profound effects on individuals and organisations. The psychologist suggested that the key to slowing down the turnover and reducing poor performance lay in fostering optimism within the team, a concept that had garnered substantial empirical support as a predictor of sales success.

Under this expert guidance, Peter integrated an optimism test into their recruitment process. This step was designed to identify individuals who possessed the requisite sales aptitude and exhibited a high degree of optimism. As the first year progressed, Peter saw a significant trend – those who scored impressively on the optimism test, in conjunction with their existing sales aptitude test results, outperformed their peers who had only passed the aptitude test. It was a breakthrough moment, highlighting the undeniable link between optimism and sales success!

By the end of the second year, Peter's observations were even more compelling. The more optimistic members of the sales team consistently outsold their pessimistic counterparts by a staggering 35%. The evidence was clear – optimism was a predictor of sales performance.

Embracing this newfound knowledge, Peter decided to take a bold step. He began actively recruiting what he termed 'super-optimists' – individuals who scored exceptionally high on the optimism test, even if they occasionally fell short on the aptitude test. The results of this experiment were astonishing.

After the first year, the super-optimists outperformed their pessimistic counterparts by a remarkable 20%. And by the end of their second year, this gap had widened to 55%.

But the benefits didn't stop there. The most optimistic salespeople were not only achieving outstanding sales results, but were also more likely to remain in their roles – twice as likely, in fact. Moreover, the team experienced a remarkable shift in their collective mindset. They became more adept at surmounting obstacles, radiated positivity and energy, and reported improved overall wellbeing.

By redefining the criteria for selecting salespeople and actively cultivating optimism within the team through targeted training, Peter and his team achieved a remarkable turnaround. They increased their sales results, retained their best talent and moved closer towards thriving.

The secret ingredient of sales success

When we think of 'successful' salespeople, what typically comes to mind is the extroverted, loud, outgoing, big personality type. I use the term 'successful' as success in this sense might be attributed to the person wearing the expensive watch. But perhaps these characteristics come once 'success' has been attained and aren't what helped them achieve it in the first place.

When you ask incredible sales leaders which attributes are common among their best salespeople, they usually use terms like diligent, confident, energetic, do-ers, focused, good with people, motivated, experienced in hitting targets and know their products.

Yet the research confirms it doesn't come down to personality type, sales ability, confidence, experience, or hunger. As the story at the start of this chapter highlights, optimism is a critical attribute for a thriving salesperson.

Optimism is a critical attribute for a thriving salesperson.

And when you think about it, this makes total sense. Optimists tend to be more positive, energetic and 'get on with it' types of people.

Typically, though, the term 'optimistic' is rarely used to describe a successful salesperson. Nor is it listed in the job description.

So, are we placing enough emphasis on the need for optimistic salespeople? Are we hiring those who are high in optimism? Are we teaching our teams to be more optimistic? Or is their development focused on technical skills? And, are we considering that low performance might come down to levels of optimism or pessimism?

Optimism sits on a continuum, so there's always room for improvement by learning actions and strategies that boost optimism within sales teams. These could be good reminders and reinforce what your salespeople are already doing.

What is optimism?

Optimism is a set of beliefs about the future. It doesn't come down to whether we see a glass as half full or half empty, although how we think does have a role. And we know that our thoughts impact our actions and how we feel.

Because optimists believe the future will be better, they tend to put more effort into the present and are less likely to give up when the going gets tough. Optimists are more innovative and creative as they like to experiment and believe that if things don't work out, they're still on the pathway to success.

Let's imagine how this might play out.

You have two salespeople on your team – one is higher in optimism and the other higher in pessimism.

When they encounter the same problem, you'll likely find that they'll respond differently. The optimist will probably think, 'This is just a bump in the road; once I get through this, things will be much easier down the track.' A pessimist facing that same challenge might believe, 'I'm not going to get through this. These challenges are just going to keep on coming. I don't think it will ever get easier, so I may as well give up now, as it's too hard.'

These two face the same problem, but they act and feel differently. And over the long term, they will experience very different outcomes.

Why do we need optimism in sales?

Optimism is the critical ingredient for salespeople to do well.

Over the past 40 years, many studies have considered the benefit of optimism for salespeople. Across a range of industries, including banking, real estate, telecommunications, customer service and automotive, optimistic salespeople outsell pessimistic salespeople by 20-40%.[1] That's a huge percentage difference determined by one factor – how optimistic your salespeople are.

So perhaps optimism breeds success, not success that breeds optimism.

Typically, pessimists are more likely to quit (including their jobs) and are less productive when challenges occur.[2] Why? Because they don't think things will get better. Optimists, on the other hand, believe their situation will improve, so they put in more effort. Optimists tend to see hurdles as opportunities, so they look for solutions. They focus on what they can control rather than what they can't, so they're more easily able to overcome setbacks.

That is why there is a strong link between optimism and resilience. Being optimistic helps people to be resilient. Ability and motivation will only ever get us so far. Salespeople must be optimistic to persist in the face of setbacks.[3]

Given their persistence, optimists tend to achieve more work-related goals, including making more money and promotions and are more successful in academia and sports.[4] They become more confident, motivated and engaged, so their optimism grows.

Optimists tend to have better quality and longer-lasting relationships because people are drawn to their positive energy. They contribute to creating a great culture within teams. This extends to strong connections with their clients and other stakeholders. The next chapter will cover the value of high-quality networks for salespeople.

In addition to the outcomes already mentioned, optimism supports wellbeing and makes people more able to deal with stress and less likely to burnout. This has a long-term positive impact on mental and physical health. When you focus on optimism, you get better salespeople and happier and healthier humans.[5]

What happens when sales leaders are optimistic?

Sales leaders need to be optimistic so they can reassure their teams during tough times and be a beacon of hope when the future looks bleak. Just as emotions are contagious, if you are a more optimistic leader, it's more likely that this will spread amongst your team.

Optimists win in challenging times.

A sales team full of optimists has a positive culture where teams are resilient, motivated, confident, adaptable and solutions orientated. They make everything better. Optimists win in challenging times.

How do you boost optimism?

As I've shown, salespeople tend to be highly optimistic. But what makes them that way? And given its importance, how do we ensure optimism stays high? Can we make it even stronger?

Researchers have uncovered differences between the thoughts, actions and feelings of optimists and pessimists. By understanding what they do differently, sales leaders can focus on strategies and actions to increase optimism.

So, what can you try?

Adopt a growth mindset

Optimists tend to see challenges as opportunities – perhaps to grow, to learn or to develop in some way. This thinking relates to Carol Dweck's concept of the growth mindset.[6] People who adopt this mindset believe their qualities, skills, intelligence and strengths can be changed and developed with effort.

This differs from those with a fixed mindset, who believe these factors can't be changed. Often, people are told to adopt a growth mindset to overcome challenges, grow from setbacks and support others to develop. But this takes more than a click of the fingers.

One way to support your team into a growth mindset is by encouraging them to set learning goals – not just performance goals related to sales targets. (A fixed mindset typically focuses on performance goals that they deem achievable. They make people feel safe as they anticipate little risk of failure.) Learning goals, however, are about increasing competence. They're about learning new skills, mastering different tasks, and relate to the desire to grow, develop or get smarter.

So, what do your team members want to learn? Perhaps it's something that might help them achieve their goals. It could be related to work, such as learning about a new piece of technology or new features of products. Or it could be something non-work related like mastering another language, taking up a musical instrument or improving their cooking skills. Whatever the learning goal, the focus is on believing they can always improve.

Use humour

Optimists often adopt humour during challenging times to distract them from a grim reality and relieve stress. When we laugh, our bodies release nitric oxide, which relaxes our blood vessels and reduces blood pressure. That is why studies have shown that people who laugh more are at less risk of major cardiovascular disease and tend to live longer.[7]

I'm not asking leaders to become standup comedians, just share a funny (and appropriate) story, clip, meme or joke.

Encourage others to do this during team meetings or via your Slack channel.

A word of caution, however, appropriate humour requires the right time, right place and the right audience. But it's a great excuse to have a laugh or some fun at work.

Be grateful

Optimists tend to be grateful for all they have rather than focused on what they don't. Because of this, they experience positive emotions, which can help manage stress, keep energy and motivation high and strengthen connections across teams. Positivity has also been shown to reduce absenteeism and increase productivity, so it's a critical ingredient for business success. Gratitude is the mega strategy for being happier, healthier, and having greater wellbeing.

Encourage your team to be grateful by cultivating an attitude of gratitude yourself. Regularly express your appreciation for your team members by calling or writing to them. Make your team's gratitude visible by building a gratitude wall. Or add an appreciation round to your meeting agendas for people to share their thanks for others.

Don't be a Pollyanna

Can you ever be too optimistic?

Unfortunately, like most things, too much optimism can come with some negatives.

People who are unjustifiably high in optimism (a Pollyanna) can focus on butterflies and rainbows without considering the challenges in their current reality. This can lead to insufficient planning and preparation for potential risks and challenges.

When sales leaders are intentionally overly optimistic during tough times, this strategy can backfire. Instead of acknowledging the challenges, they set the expectation that teams must suck it up, not admit that things are tough or how they're truly feeling. This erodes psychological safety and negatively impacts performance, as discussed in Chapter Five.

The idea is that we all want to be realistically optimistic – that's having a good dose of optimism with a splash of pessimism.

Summary

- Optimism relates to how we think, impacting our actions and feelings.
- Optimists outsell pessimists by 20-40%.
- Success doesn't breed optimism. Optimism breeds success.
- Optimism impacts performance and helps us to be resilient and well.
- Our aim is for realistic optimism, not extreme optimism.

CHAPTER EIGHT

FOSTERING HIGH QUALITY NETWORKS

Other People Matter.

– Chris Peterson

Ben was always a high performer in his sales role at one of the country's leading banks. His numbers were consistently great, and he was a standout within his workplace and across the entire industry. But behind his impressive sales figures, another story was unfolding.

His fiercely competitive approach had helped get him so far. But that competitiveness also played out with his team. Rather than viewing his colleagues as allies, Ben regarded them as rivals in a relentless race to the top. Rachel, Ben's manager, was well aware of this aspect of his personality as she had received numerous complaints from team members about Ben's behaviour.

Recently, Ben's competitive nature had taken an unpleasant turn. He was frequently described as aggressive and rude towards his colleagues and other support staff. He deflected blame onto others, rarely took responsibility for his mistakes, and often belittled his peers. Worst of all, Ben had encroached into his colleagues' territories and undermined their relationships with clients.

Ben's actions were consistently at odds with the group's core values, yet his disruptive behaviour went unchecked. He continued to be rewarded for the numbers he delivered. To make matters worse, Ben was even crowned the company's Salesperson of the Year at the annual conference.

Rachel grappled with this dilemma. She wanted to foster a cohesive team where mutual support and respect thrived. However, she had chosen to turn a blind eye to Ben's misconduct. After all, his remarkable sales performance had contributed significantly to the team's overall success, making Rachel look great in the eyes of her leaders. Ben's clients consistently praised his work, so it was difficult for Rachel to reprimand him for one aspect of his behaviour while praising him for another. She was torn as Ben was a critical contributor to the team's numbers so she didn't want to lose him and be left with a huge hole to fill.

However, Ben's antics were taking a toll on the team. Team meetings, which were once characterised by camaraderie, celebrating successes, sharing of losses, and collaborative discussions on strategies, had become tense and hostile whenever Ben was present. Ben stopped participating and rarely shared insights or strategies, fearing that his colleagues might exploit them to their advantage. Instead, he spent much of the meeting time complaining or glued to his phone.

The team's respect for Rachel waned as Ben's poor behaviour persisted. They were disheartened by the stark differences in her treatment of team members. The workplace environment had turned toxic, collaboration dwindled, and the team was losing sight of their shared goals, instead wasting valuable time venting frustrations about Ben and Rachel.

Despite Ben's stellar performance, the team overall consistently fell short of their targets. Employee engagement scores plummeted, morale reached an all-time low, energy levels waned, fatigue increased, and team members began calling in sick more frequently. A couple of team members decided to leave, and in their exit interviews, they cited Ben, but more significantly, Rachel's inaction as their reasons for departing.

Rachel knew she could no longer avoid the issue. It was time to address Ben's behaviour head-on and concentrate on rebuilding strong connections within the team. The future of the team's success depended on it.

What are high-quality networks?

As humans, our brains are wired to connect with others. Every salesperson knows that achieving your KPIs depends on their relationships with their clients.

But excellent salespeople – those who are engaged and highest performing – know that other relationships are instrumental in their success, too. These may include team members, leaders, and support teams, up, down and across their organisations. And don't forget the industry networks, such as coaches, mentors and trainers.

Success comes down to the quality of your network.

Your network might be wide, but your success comes down to the quality of your network, not the quantity. Fewer but more meaningful and valuable relationships are more important than a large number of superficial or shallow connections.

The best connections we can have are with energisers. These people are positive, trustworthy, enjoy other people and see opportunities even in challenging situations.[1] They sound a bit like optimists, don't they? They offer information, share best practices, provide mentoring or support, give feedback and challenge you. Energisers show you what's important in life and what we can learn from.

Energisers differ from drainers who criticise or blame. They don't share ideas. They miss their commitments, focus on challenges instead of opportunities and don't show care for others. Ben was a drainer. They make us feel unsafe because they judge, criticise, intimidate or bully. Yet we know that feeling safe is fundamental to successful relationships.

Although drainers can still achieve their targets, they don't benefit anyone (even themselves) long term because their interactions deplete us. We avoid them because they drain our energy and create toxicity. You know the interactions I'm talking about! And after those bruising encounters, we expend even more effort and time trying to understand why someone would treat us this way.

We have high-quality connections with energisers because they give us energy. Jane Dutton, from the University of Michigan, is a leading researcher on relationships at work. She says high-quality connections occur when we feel a sense of positive regard, mutuality or vitality.[2] We're drawn to interactions that light us up because energy acts like a magnet. We seek them out,

We're drawn to interactions that light us up.

particularly when we're tired or downcast from a pitch that didn't go well.

The quality of our connections and the energy they provide positively or negatively impact people and workplaces.

Why are high-quality sales networks important?

A salesperson's long-term success depends on the quality of their client relationships. When the quality is higher, clients are more likely to trust you, so it's easier and more likely that you will make a sale. Positive experiences mean they tend to repeat business and become loyal to your brand or organisation.

When the relationship is strong, you're more likely to receive referrals from clients who are highly satisfied with your product or service. When an issue occurs, your client is more likely to reach out and communicate their concerns, and you can facilitate a smoother resolution.

Customers who feel connected to you are willing to provide feedback, so you know what's working well, what's not and what needs to improve. You stand out from your competitors. High-quality relationships are sticky, so clients won't look elsewhere for products or services. Building long-term relationships gives salespeople a sense of fulfilment and satisfaction and certainly helps them achieve their targets.

But salespeople can also benefit from relationships beyond their clients, including connections with their team and networks across their organisations, industries and communities. These support them to be engaged, achieve more, and thrive.

Since we spend so much time at work, having strong relationships with our colleagues makes sense. These relationships motivate us, making us more productive, energised and engaged. And that's what we need right now. Teams that work together are higher performing and tend to achieve more. In his book *The Five Dysfunctions of a Team*, Patrick Lencioni wrote that teamwork is 'the ultimate competitive advantage because it is so powerful and rare'.[3]

A Gallup study showed that you're seven times more likely to be engaged if you have a best friend at work.[4] Relationships at work drive job satisfaction. When you feel you belong, your team cares for you, and your environment is energising, you increase your commitment to your workplace and are less likely to consider leaving. When others hear about the supportive culture, they also want to join your team. If people don't feel like they fit in and their environment is depleting, they tend to leave.

Turnover is typically high in sales teams. As we're currently fighting a war on talent, you want your people to feel like they belong. Losing salespeople is particularly costly if it's your best performers. Best doesn't mean those bringing in the biggest revenue, but rather those high performers who are positive contributors to your culture too. Turnover hurts sales numbers as, typically, roles sit empty for some time or aren't replaced, so client relationships aren't nurtured or are neglected.

Losing salespeople is particularly costly if it's your best performers.

The better your relationships, the more positive emotions you experience. This is essential for sales teams, as the happier you are, the more likely you are to make a sale.[5] When you have great connections at work, you are more often in a positive state, making you better at problem-solving and more creative and innovative. That helps your organisation to stand out from its competitors.[6] The positivity that stems from relationships can also put you on an upward spiral of growth and development because you are more likely to share knowledge, ideas and different ways of doing things when you feel good.

Positive emotions are highly beneficial for your wellbeing and mental and physical health. When you connect with others, your body releases the feel-good hormone oxytocin, which reduces stress or anxiety. This happens best when you laugh.

Over time, you will build skills from positive emotions, which help you to be more resilient (see Chapter Six on Resilience). So, when your next challenge strikes, you're better equipped to cope well. What's more, you'll feel supported because you are surrounded by people who care for you, so you'll be more compassionate towards your peers in their times of need. This is particularly important in sales roles because you need your colleagues to help pick you up when you've been knocked down and encourage you to keep moving towards your goals. You want to celebrate your successes with your colleagues too. Celebrating is no fun on your own!

Positivity can help reduce conflict among team members. When negative feedback or criticism is shared, it's more likely to be addressed when you have quality relationships in your team.

We've spoken about burnout being on the rise in workplaces. According to researchers Emily and Amelia Nagoski, increasing kindness and connection is one way to prevent it.[7] The imbalance between demands and resources can lead to burnout, so if demands aren't decreasing, we need to increase our resources. These include social support from our colleagues.

It's pretty clear why high-quality connections at work are important for salespeople. It was, therefore, surprising to learn that the number one struggle experienced by

Australian workers is dealing with other people.[8] The Wellbeing Lab study didn't distinguish who these people are, but we can assume some will be in your work networks.

Poor working relationships are costly for individuals, teams and organisations. There's little doubt you will have experienced toxicity in your workplace at some point. In fact, 98% of people have experienced uncivil and rude behaviour at work.[9] Leaders know that incivility is bad, but few leaders understand the cost of rude team members or turning a blind eye to poor behaviour. Let it be known that disrespect has a direct hit on your bottom line.

A range of negative consequences come when we interact with drainers over time. These include decreased engagement, poorer wellbeing, greater stress, less resilience, more dissatisfaction, and decreased performance. Basically, these are the opposite of everything that high-quality connections bring.

Few leaders understand the cost of rude team members.

Toxic people cause toxicity within a group. It's a culture killer. When team members are overwhelmed by poor behaviour, they become less productive and put less effort into their work. They respond negatively to the rude behaviour, which creates a vicious cycle. They eventually spend less time at work or quit, as they don't want to be around that person. The greater risk here is that the rest of your team will leave too.[10]

Research has shown that customers are less likely to buy from a company that has an employee perceived as rude, whether the rudeness is directed at them or at other employees.[11] No one likes to see others treated badly, so drainers can inadvertently damage your brand and reputation. Conversely, we can't tolerate rude or uncivil behaviour from customers towards our salespeople. As sales leaders, your role is to protect them.

What's the leader's role in building high quality connections?

Every interaction, big or small, can boost or deplete energy. Given that energy is one of our most finite resources, we choose to bring the best or worst out in others. As a leader, your choice will significantly impact your team, as energy is contagious.

If you want your team to be full of energisers, this starts with you. You are responsible for modelling and fostering your team members' relationships with one another.

That includes ensuring you have the right type of people on your team, which means no 'brilliant jerks'. (A term both Atlassian and Netflix use to describe workers who deliver results but make life miserable for those around them.)

While these people may excel in sales, drainers will be detrimental to your team's success in the long run as they don't share your values. They shouldn't be hired in the first place as they will cause much pain and, at worst, the loss of some of your star performers.

Deal with them quickly if they're already on your team. It can be difficult to make these decisions (as Rachel found), as their high performance can cloud your perceptions and impede the right choice for the team overall. Ultimately, though, they need to go.

Leaders play a role in creating an environment where high-quality relationships can thrive. This is where you need to look at how you communicate, how you interact, how meetings are run, when social events take place, how you share wins and losses, how you support others, and how you hold people to account for their results and the behaviour expected of them. It is particularly so in hybrid or fully remote environments. In addition to rewarding the achievement of KPIs, good organisational citizenship behaviour must also be acknowledged.

Make sure that you haven't inadvertently set up your team to compete against one another to motivate them. Some leaders believe their people work harder when they compete against one another, but the result is a cutthroat culture.

Thriving sales teams are connected and see themselves as one, working together for a common goal – not as individuals working alone in pursuit of their own KPIs. Your team will go further when they have high-quality connections but are positively competitive, so they feel challenged and incentivised to work harder.

> The quality of our networks impacts the outcomes we achieve.

How well you, your sales team or your organisation thrive largely depends on the quality of your workplace connections that can drive competitive advantage. [12]

How can you build high quality networks?

Jane Dutton reminds us that the quality of our networks impacts the outcomes we achieve.[13] So, leaders want to invest time and effort into improving them. We can influence the quality of the relationships our team has at work.

We have already spoken about the importance of trust in building stronger relationships in Chapter Five.

When we celebrate and acknowledge others' strengths, we show them they're valued and appreciated, as outlined in Chapter Four.

So, what else can you try?

Engage respectfully

To increase the quality of our relationships, we need to engage respectfully with others. This is particularly important in the leader/worker relationship. Small acts matter here, like being interested in people's lives outside of work, offering praise for a job well done (no matter how big or small), or simply being present when interacting. It might also look like putting away your phone and laptop while in a meeting and focusing on the person. This signals that you are listening and care about the conversation.

Replace judgement with curiosity

Humans tend to rush to judgements about people. These are shortcuts to save time and figure out if a person is a friend or foe. Yet our conclusions are typically wrong and hinder the quality of our relationships. In these moments, researcher Brené Brown asks that rather than being judgemental, we be curious.[14] Assume that people are doing the best they can with what they have at that moment. Rather than judging, slow down and ask what might be happening. Offer support, expose some of your own vulnerabilities and share some of the responsibility for their situation.

Play

How can you inject more fun into your team's working day? It's a great way to build connection and resilience and destress. Play could be formal or informal, or scheduled or unscheduled. And could be in the form of team activities, social events, celebrations, fundraising or volunteering opportunities. Or it could be coming up with playlists, running cooking competitions, doing daily brain teasers, sharing jokes or memes, or setting up an exercise club. If your workplace allows it, set up spaces for people to share meals and have games or ping-pong tables available to enable people to connect informally. When we have fun with others, we see them differently.

Summary

- Incivility is on the rise in workplaces, and leaders have a role in fostering curiosity in relationships.
- High-quality relationships light us up, while low-quality relationships drain us.
- It is a choice to be an energiser or a drainer.
- Relationships with clients, team members and leaders are fundamental to sales success.

CHAPTER NINE

ACHIEVING GOALS AND PURPOSE

> *People with goals succeed because*
> *they know where they are going.*
>
> – Earl Nightingale

In the health sector, a team sells medical imaging equipment to hospitals and surgeons. They used to be one of the highest performers in their organisation and a leader in their industry, too. However, recently, the team seemed to have lost their spark. Their organisation had undergone immense change, and the team's motivation had withered away.

The product teams that the sales team relied upon had suffered significant headcount reductions, causing a lag in product development and innovation. The team no longer held their coveted position at the forefront of the industry. Their products were no longer outshining their competitors. Sales figures began to dip, and the pressure on their leader, Steve, to deliver grew exponentially. Senior leadership increasingly scrutinised their performance. What's more, Steve's boss had begun attending their team meetings, and the CEO insisted on reviewing their weekly sales reports, which conveyed to Steve a lack of trust in his ability to manage his team effectively.

Steve's team was aware of the mounting pressure on their leader. Coupled with their feelings of overwhelm and insecurity regarding meeting their targets, the team began to sense their motivation declining. The decline started with one individual and quickly spread like wildfire. The team's energy and passion waned noticeably. Team activities and meetings became lifeless, and people seemed increasingly distracted when they were in the office. Even their enthusiasm during client engagements dwindled. Over time, Steve watched helplessly as several of his star performers were lured away by rival organisations offering irresistible incentives to jump ship.

Despite Steve's mounting concerns, his CEO steadfastly refused to increase bonuses, instead intensifying the pressure on Steve to meet targets with a reduced team. The weight of this responsibility was taking a toll on Steve's wellbeing, and he found himself grasping for solutions. In a desperate bid to regain control, Steve unwittingly resorted to controlling his team's every move. He demanded that every team member share their calendars, wanting to micromanage their daily activities, including all their meetings. Working from home was no longer an option, and he insisted that team members be *physically present in the office, when not with clients. Training and social events were cancelled as the sole priority became achieving their sales goals.*

As months rolled by, the team looked nothing like their former peak-performance selves. Their best team members had departed, and those left were disengaged, exhausted, cynical, highly stressed, demotivated and far from hitting their targets. Steve was on the brink of burnout and felt helpless about how to rebuild his team and reignite their motivation.

What is motivation?

Having a team of highly motivated individuals committed and focused on achieving their goals would have to be the ultimate for any leader. It's more so for sales leaders, where motivation is one of the most important traits of a salesperson.

Motivation is that inner drive or desire that spurs us to take action and work toward our goals. It can also support the persistence needed to achieve what we set out to do. So, motivation is a powerful force in shaping who we are and how we behave. Yet it typically ebbs and flows. Consider New Year's Resolutions. Despite best intentions, less than 10% of people see them through.[1]

Sales team motivation decreases when their environments are challenged by changing market conditions, a client's increased expectations or other competitive products or services.

It's often thought that money drives motivation for salespeople. If they are paid well, they will have a greater drive to meet and even exceed their goals. But that thinking is somewhat outdated. In reality, incentives don't last long and can mean little when the environment is challenging. And despite compensation being used as a lever to stop people from leaving, it typically has a low success rate. It's also hard for leaders to continue to dangle money as higher payments will have to cease at some point. So, money is not a sustainable strategy to motivate your team.

Money is not a sustainable strategy to motivate your team.

Consider when you've been tempted to move to a different organisation for a big incentive. Many people don't go. Why? What keeps them with their current employer? And what does that suggest about motivation?

When trying to find out more about motivation, there are no better people to turn to than Richard Ryan and Ed Deci, two psychologists and leading researchers on the subject. They found that motivation sits on a spectrum that includes three different groups, as outlined in Figure 7.[2]

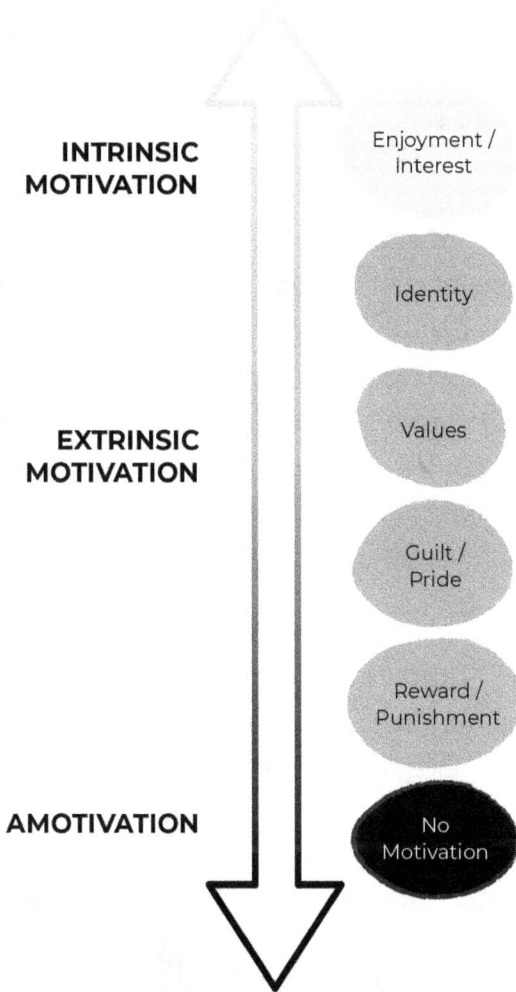

Figure 7: Motivation continuum (adapted from Ryan & Deci, 2000)

At one end are people who aren't motivated. Next are those who are extrinsically motivated by a reward or punishment, or by a sense of guilt or feeling they should do something.

Further along, people are motivated extrinsically as their actions align with their values or identity. And at the other end of the spectrum, people are intrinsically motivated when they do something because they want to for pure enjoyment, interest and satisfaction.

This continuum model explains why money only ever motivates people to a certain point. Once salespeople are paid enough, they give their best at work for other reasons. It helps us understand why people don't go when offered big cheques to move to their competitors. And perhaps why some of the wealthiest people in the world, like Jeff Bezos, Bill Gates, or Warren Buffet, continue to get out of bed each day and work hard.

When I've asked salespeople at the top of their game what drives them to be the best, money is never discussed. When I've asked about leaders who have been the most motivating, they've never mentioned those who offer rewards. Money serves a purpose in meeting our lower-order needs like security, housing, food and health, but it doesn't mean much once these are taken care of.

So, there must be other factors that drive salespeople.

Often, salespeople are motivated when they do work they're interested in or proud of, become the best they can be, or seek recognition from their peers. Motivation can also increase when people collaborate with others they like to achieve their goals. It might be about having flexibility in how they work. Motivation can also come down to the *why* behind someone's work – when they understand how their role contributes to something or someone outside themselves.

On the motivation continuum, each of these reasons sits closer to the top of the band and further from things like money or punishment. That means these are much bigger driving forces and explains why some teams aren't motivated when they're paid well.

In this light, motivation differs greatly from the old stick and carrot approach, where leaders tried to motivate others through punishment, public recognition or offering big bonuses. This approach can work in some instances, such as if a task is particularly boring or a behaviour needs to be controlled.

In their research, Ryan and Deci also uncovered that we are more and better motivated when three of our needs are met: competence, autonomy and relatedness.[3]

Competence relates to our desire to build knowledge and develop skills to feel capable in our roles. We want to work for employers who will grow us to be our best. We don't want to feel we're consistently up against tough challenges, but rather that we have mastery to overcome them. And we also want to see a long-term career path at our employer, one where we are continuously advancing ourselves and not restricted in how much we can develop.

> **A clear sense of purpose is a powerful motivator.**

When we feel autonomous in our roles, we have control and choice over how we do our jobs, how we go about our roles, when we work or who we work with. This helps us to feel energised and satisfied.

Relatedness speaks to the innate desire that we all have to belong and have strong connections with those around us.

When leaders meet these needs, people are intrinsically motivated. They enjoy their work as it is inherently satisfying. However, when frustrated, it is harder for people to be intrinsically motivated, and they are more likely to be disengaged and depleted over time.

Another big driver of intrinsic motivation is having a sense of meaning and purpose in your role.[4] Identifying this can influence every aspect of your life, including your career choice, goals and daily actions to achieve them. A clear sense of purpose is a powerful motivator. Some examples of organisations that stand for what they believe in are Apple, Tesla, Vision Australia and AIA Australia. These groups have a clear *why*, which motivates their teams to reach a common goal and go the extra mile.

Why is (intrinsic) motivation important?

Salespeople typically have clear objectives. A budget is set at the start of the year or quarter, and you need to hit it. That's a big advantage, unlike other areas of organisations where outcomes are less specific.

Although the KPI might be known, the leader must ensure the sales team is motivated to achieve it. Ultimately, motivation is the driving force behind achieving goals and impacts success. When teams are highly motivated, they're more likely to set ambitious targets and be driven to achieve them.

Motivated sales teams have energy, passion and enthusiasm. They're more productive because they have a hunger to achieve their objectives. This supports them to persist and adapt to an increasingly complex sales environment. Motivated individuals are more engaged, as they tend to be focused and accountable. Sales teams achieve better results when they're working towards a common goal. When 'we're all in this together', they tend to support one another more. Higher team motivation leads to stronger relationships with customers.[5]

Like emotions, motivation is contagious, rippling throughout your team and creating a productive and positive work environment that encourages better collaboration within and across the organisation.

A group of intrinsically motivated salespeople won't consider or be tempted by other roles. You'll have created a team culture that retains and attracts quality talent.

They are a flight risk if they're disconnected from the company's purpose, feel overwhelmed by the pressure to perform, or their unmet needs. They're no doubt experiencing thoughts of finding grass that is greener elsewhere. They can become cynical about you or your organisation and voice their opinions. And just as positivity is contagious, so is negativity, which can spread even more rapidly.

What responsibility do leaders have to motivate their team?

The challenge for leaders is uncovering what motivates the team.

If you focus on the wrong things, you risk demotivating them. When some leaders are unsure, they default to the 'stick' approach, ramping up the pressure and punishing teams by taking away what matters most – flexibility and autonomy. This only increases stress and frustration. Some leaders revert to micromanagement to control the situation. They rule a line through social events or training and development opportunities and put more pressure on the team by letting the CEO sit in on their weekly sales meetings.

This approach doesn't get leaders far, and we have repeatedly seen it fail. It's counterintuitive to what we know motivates people. Such actions send good people looking elsewhere for roles.

The good news is that you can motivate your team without taking away what's important to them or by threatening punishment or offering rewards. Meeting their needs of *competence, autonomy, relatedness and purpose* doesn't have to cost a thing!

Start by ensuring individuals understand your organisation's purpose and their role in achieving it. Salespeople need to know the impact of their product or service on their clients. When they experience this, they are more motivated to work harder as they realise that what they do contributes to something greater than themselves.

They will find meaning in their role when they can tie their purpose (what gets them out of bed each day) with the organisation's purpose. It sets up a clear pathway to success and is particularly important for support staff – not just the front line. Understanding your purpose pulls you through challenging times.[6] Some people will even work for less money if they are doing meaningful work like those at not-for-profits.

How do we motivate our team?

We know motivation is important, but how do we achieve that when times are tough, teams shrink, markets fluctuate, clients are uneasy, and the pressure ramps up?

You know that intrinsic motivation is achieved when people are competent in their job, have autonomy in their role, experience a sense of belonging and are connected to their purpose. The first step in this process would be to ask your people what each aspect looks and feels like. They will mean different things to different people.

Chapter Eight covered how to strengthen connections in our networks, which connects to the relatedness element discussed here. Similarly, Chapter Five on Trust and Psychological Safety also focused on the foundational elements essential for high-quality connections.

So, what else can you try?

Uncover purpose

When President John F. Kennedy visited NASA for the first time in 1962, he asked a cleaner what his job was. The cleaner replied, 'I'm helping to put a man on the moon'. This often-quoted story is a great example of how every role has meaning. Leaders need to support teams to uncover meaning in their roles. In the words of another famous American, Simon Sinek, we must 'start with why'. Ensure your team knows what they're doing and why they're doing it. They will be more willing to go the extra mile and support others along the journey when they know why they are coming to work.

Build competence

To motivate and retain your talent, provide them with opportunities to learn, grow and develop in their roles. This doesn't only have to be formal, like attending workshops; it might take the form of role-shadowing, allowing them to rotate their roles or responsibilities, providing them with challenging work, or supporting them with a coach or mentor. Additionally, you can provide regular feedback (both positive and constructive), which specifically reinforces what they're doing well and where they need to improve. Create a feedback culture where it's something that everyone can do for one another.

Offer autonomy

Autonomy can be achieved in roles by giving people flexibility. That doesn't mean working away from the office – for some in retail, that's impossible. Autonomy might mean flexible start, break and end times. Or it might be about choosing who you work with or the type of work you do. Consider offering your teams free time to explore something that interests them. Several workplaces (like Google and Atlassian) allow their teams to spend a percentage of their time working on projects of their choosing. This gives an element of autonomy and can lead to greater creativity and innovation of new ideas, products or services.

Summary

- Motivation is one of the most important traits of a salesperson.
- Motivation ebbs and flows and can decrease when we're in challenging environments.
- Motivation is a continuum from extrinsic to intrinsic.
- Salespeople are only motivated by money to a certain point. They are highly motivated when we satisfy their needs for competence, autonomy, relatedness and purpose.

PART 3

Applying your learning

At this point, you've learned much of what there is to know about the STRONG principles.

Perhaps you recognised some of the strategies. Maybe they align with how you lead. If so, that's great news and hopefully a good reminder of the incredible ways you're already leading. Keep doing what you're doing!

Yet perhaps some of the principles may be new to you. As I said initially, STRONG isn't rocket science, even though it's based on science. Intuitively, all the elements should make sense. But there might be a few that you're not fully adopting. Perhaps you haven't encountered them before; you're unsure of the *how* behind each, or maybe due to factors outside your control, they're not encouraged or fully supported as ways to lead in your organisation.

If, like other sales leaders I work with, you want to engage your team, achieve better results and thrive in the process, then you should be convinced that STRONG is the way to do that.

But knowledge is no good if it's not put into practice.

Which parts of STRONG will you focus on?

You can't do them all at once, so it's best to focus on one or two to begin. Once you've mastered those, come back to the others when the time is right.

So, which will you choose?

With greater understanding, let's reflect again on STRONG.

As you did earlier, rate yourself out of 5 across each of the STRONG principles.

How STRONG are you?

Let's see how well you are applying the STRONG principles with your team.

In the Agreement column, rate yourself across each element from 1 (Strongly disagree), 2 (Disagree), 3 (Neither agree nor disagree), 4 (Agree), to 5 (Strongly agree).

STRONG principle	Description	Agreement (1-5)
Strengths	I know the strengths of my team members and regularly look at ways to grow and develop them, and manage their weaknesses	
Trust and Psychological Safety	I have built a team that trusts each other, with a culture where team members can make mistakes, provide feedback, and share and learn from one another	
Resilience	I ensure that my team has the skills to cope well with challenges and grow from struggles, setbacks or change	
Optimism	I help my team develop an optimistic mindset so they are action-oriented, problem-solvers, energetic and positive	
Networks	I support my team in building high-quality connections with one another, our clients and stakeholders	
Goals and Purpose	I meet the needs of my team so they are intrinsically motivated to achieve our goals and purpose.	

- Where are you doing well?
- Which STRONG principles are a strength of your leadership?
- Where are you scoring low?
- Has this changed from when you completed this earlier?

Now, choose the one or two elements that will help you engage your top talent, achieve greater results and thrive. Focusing on all at once will only set you up to fail.

Don't choose the areas where you score the lowest. It's far better to consider the principles that your leadership needs to focus on to achieve your goals, and what your team needs to be at their best.

Your chosen elements will form part of your new leadership development plan. It should also include the areas where you're doing well so they're reinforced and not forgotten. Keep referring back to them. You might also find that some take longer to grasp, and those you're doing well in might dip temporarily, depending on what's going on around you.

Remember, the STRONG model can stick with you throughout your leadership. You might add to it, but the basic elements will last forever.

CHAPTER TEN

MAKING CHANGE STICK

Motivation is what gets you started.
Habit is what keeps you going.
– Jim Rohn

You've just spent three days in workshops on how to be a better sales leader. Or perhaps you've been coached for the past six months on changes needed to be your best. Or maybe you've just finished reading a book (STRONG!) that covers the strategies for you and your team to be at their best. Yet despite your greatest intentions, a new day rolls around and you find yourself back at your desk, responding to emails, making calls to customers and answering the questions of your team between back-to-back meetings. All the new information you've gained gets pushed to the back of your mind as demands pile up.

One day, you find yourself in a difficult conversation – exactly like the one discussed during your training. You think, 'I know I am meant to act differently here, but I can't remember how', so you just use the tactics you've always used. Or you are considering how to take your team's performance to the next level at the start of the new year. When the pressure continues to increase, rather than reaching for tactics that will help, you revert to what you've always done because it's what you know. Over time, everything you learned from your training is a dim memory.

So, you don't improve. You stay the same. Or you get worse. Your leadership doesn't change, so neither does your impact. Or it gets worse. Your team doesn't become any more engaged. They stay the same. Or they get worse. Your results don't improve, so you lose your best talent. You are nowhere near thriving and a lot closer to burning out.

Nothing will get better unless you do. Nothing will change unless you do.

Change is hard

Change requires a great deal of determination and effort – especially positive behaviour change.

How to create long-lasting change is still a big topic for research. As mentioned in Chapter Nine, we can't rely on motivation alone to stick with change because drive tends to wane over time and only gets us so far.

Some studies have uncovered ways to make change easier and ensure we're more likely to succeed.

At this point, you know the one or two STRONG principles you want to focus on next.

We can't rely on motivation alone.

This book has suggested actions on *how* to boost each of these six elements. If you look back, you'll see them summarised at the end of each chapter. Every strategy has worked for others, which is why they're evidence-backed. But it's not an exhaustive list. There are lots of other activities you could try.

Do they fit?

Not every strategy will suit you and your team. This is where you need to understand the characteristics of your team – who they are, their personalities, the specific work they do, the strengths they have, the goals they're aiming for and how they typically operate. This speaks to the idea of person-activity-fit, where we choose activities that fit ourselves and our teams to increase our chances of success.[1] This approach means choosing what you think you should do, not what your boss or someone else in the organisation wants you to do.

Are they tiny and specific?

We've all been there before. We attempt an exciting behaviour change, so we set goals that are too big, expect results too quickly, or go at them too hard, and set ourselves up for failure.

You should certainly have ambitious dreams, but the way to achieve them is to start small. When we break big actions into tiny steps, we're more likely to do them.[2] You're better off committing to something small and sticking to it for longer than taking on something big that requires too much effort and time. Remember, little steps taken every day, amount to big change over the long term. Tiny is mighty!

Tiny is mighty!

So, what's the smallest activity you could do to boost your chosen STRONG pillar? Challenge yourself as to whether it's small enough. Remember, this action has to slot somewhere into your already full life, so it can't require hours. That is also why you are better off focusing on one or two elements of STRONG that are most valuable to you and your team now.

Your goal needs to be very specific. Rather than committing to 'focus on your team's strengths', consider what action will most likely achieve your desired result. Perhaps it might be providing feedback during your one-on-ones or assigning team tasks to the person with the required strengths.

Can you create a habit?

Studies have shown that when we want to be successful with change, we need to repeat actions so they turn into habits. Our days are made up of a series of habits (both good and bad). We wake up, exercise, shower, get dressed, drink coffee, eat breakfast, commute to the office, sit at our desks, turn on our computers. Researchers from Duke University found that approximately 40% to 45% of our daily actions are automatic behaviours or habits.[3] That means for around six hours each day, we're doing something without even deciding to do it.

Habits are our business as usual. They're just part of what we do and who we are. Habits come from repetition and practice. In his book *Atomic Habits*, James Clear writes that people who build better habits get better results.[4]

So, to implement change successfully, consider how to form a new habit. Behavioural scientist BJ Fogg says, 'Tiny actions work best when we want to do them, we can do them, and we have a nudge to prompt ourselves'.[5] Fogg researched habits and discovered that behaviour change occurs when motivation, ability and a prompt converge as shown in Figure 8.

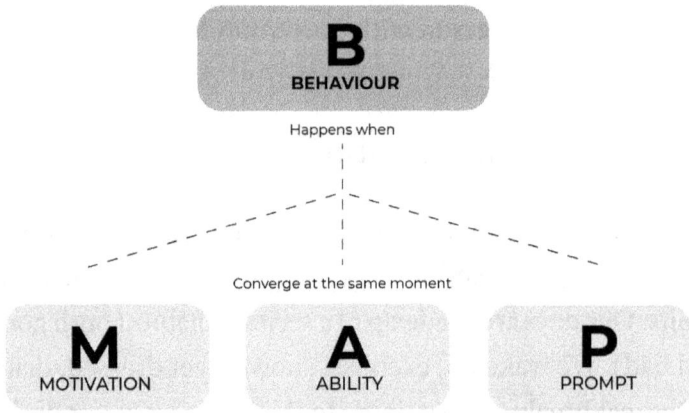

Figure 8: Behaviour Change model (adapted from Fogg, 2019)

To be *motivated,* be sure the change is something you want to do – not something you think you should or believe is the right thing. If you're not excited by the change, it will be hard to stick to.

When motivation, ability and prompt come together, behaviour begins to change.

We need the *ability* to action the new behaviour. This is about knowledge or skills; becoming the world's best cyclist would be hard if you didn't know how to ride a bike.

And finally, our brains need a *prompt* to remind us to act; otherwise, it won't happen. That might be a certain time, like the start of a team meeting, or when you're with a particular person or in a specific location.

When motivation, ability and prompt come together, behaviour begins to change. If we don't want to do something, don't know how to, or don't think we can, that's a recipe for disaster.

Other behaviour change researchers suggest we should reward ourselves for taking action.[6] (Now we're talking!) A reward tells our brain that this action or process is worth remembering. It can be anything you like, but it's strongly suggested you choose a healthy option like a coffee, a nutritious treat or participating in a hobby instead of alcohol or chocolate.

Following these suggestions will reprogram some of your routines and over time, you will have formed a new habit and succeeded with your desired change.

What are you learning?

Try some of the strategies with your team and see how they go. Some will work, and some may not. That's because nothing is ever truly proven. Research only ever tells us what works for most people, most of the time. Be your own guinea pig and test these strategies yourself. Play with them, pull them apart and shape them so they best work for you and your team.

As you try these new activities, know that you will make mistakes, encounter setbacks and bump up against your limitations.[7] That's what it means to be human. So be kind to yourself and see these as opportunities to learn.

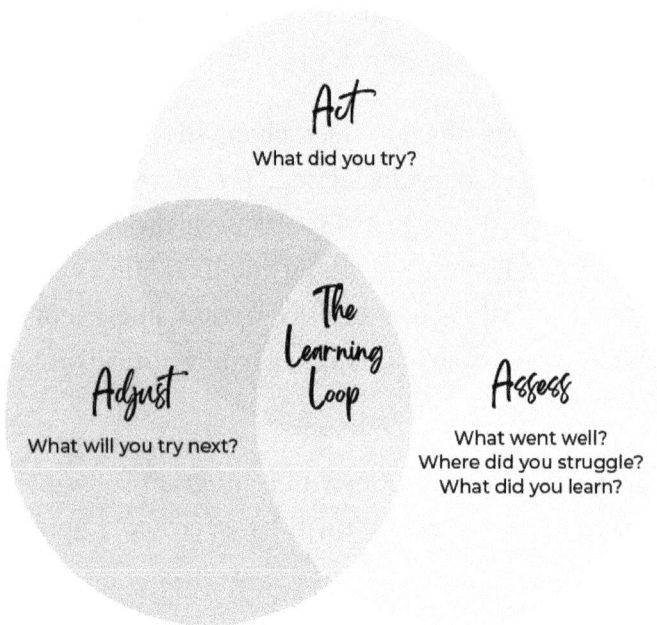

Figure 9: The Learning Loop (adapted from McQuaid & Melville, 2019)

In Chapter Five on Trust and Psychological Safety, I referred to The Learning Loop (Figure 9) that helps us act, assess our efforts and adjust them for the future so we're more likely to be successful over the long term.[8]

The loop comprises a series of questions to answer by yourself and/or with your team.

- What did you try?
- What went well?
- Where did you struggle?
- What did you learn?
- What will you try next?

I've no doubt this journey will be messy, uncomfortable, difficult, awkward and rarely perfect. That's what learning feels like when we're outside our comfort zones and in the growth arena. But if you permit yourself to fail, you'll be more likely to tweak your actions and keep persevering than give up.

Summary

- Change is hard, particularly positive behaviour change.
- To make desired changes more successful, consider their fit, how tiny they are, how they can become habits, and what your reward will be.
- The Learning Loop reminds us that there's growth in failure.

CHAPTER ELEVEN

EMBEDDING CHANGE

The bigger picture

This book has focused on sales leaders and the STRONG principles that will support you to engage your team, achieve more and thrive. But it's important to remember that the responsibility for delivering on those outcomes doesn't just sit with you.

You are part of a system. At work, we are individuals, team members and part of the organisation overall.

So, when you set out to achieve better outcomes, know that this isn't a solo endeavour. The whole system needs to be considered to embed change fully. That means looking at the 'Me', 'We' and 'Us' levels of organisations as illustrated

It's hard to thrive if your team or workplace aren't also thriving.

in Figure 10.[1] It's hard to thrive if your team or workplace aren't also thriving.

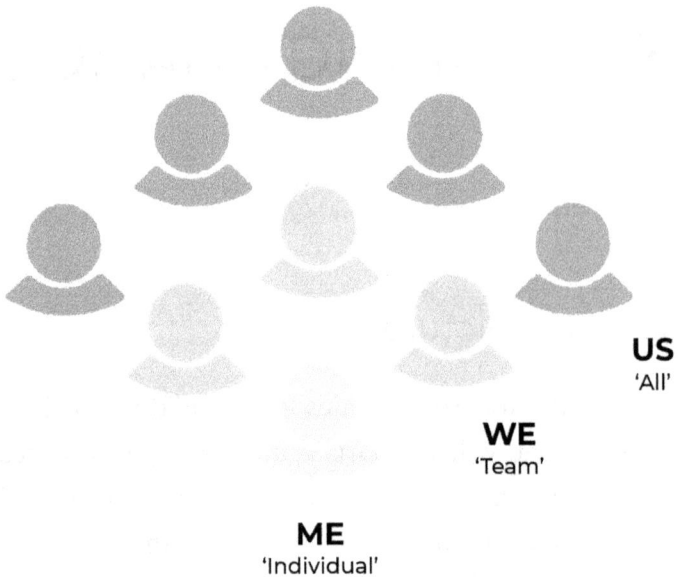

US
'All'

WE
'Team'

ME
'Individual'

Figure 10: Me, We, Us model (adapted from Jarden, 2015)

Me

At the 'Me' level are your actions as an individual contributor and don't involve others, for example, identifying your strengths. This book hasn't focused on this level – that's saved for the future!

We

At the 'We' level are activities that require multiple people, and typically a leader and their team. You will most likely undertake these with your team in a group format. For example, it could involve expressing gratitude in team meetings. Much of what's captured in this book is aimed at this level.

Us

The 'Us' level looks at the culture of your organisation. These elements tend to touch everyone and encompass the policies, processes, rules, routines and rituals that define your workplace. It also includes your vision or mission. An activity here might involve crafting a diversity and inclusion policy. Like the 'Me' level, the 'Us' level is not the focus of this book. That will come later.

To become STRONG, we need to consider all three levels in a top-down and bottom-up approach. As the leader, you set the tone of your organisation's culture and must model the actions your workplace wishes to see. Your behaviour is contagious and spreads easily through the web of connections that surround you. That's why the focus is on you, as the leader, to begin.

This work is never done, and change won't happen overnight. But as you work through the process, you will learn new ways of leading and gain new knowledge about yourself and your leadership.

Now it's over to you!

Summary

- To successfully embed change, we need to consider the different levels of our systems: Me, We and Us.
- All three levels are essential to become fully STRONG. Start here with We.
- Change won't happen overnight, but the journey is worth it.

ABOUT THE AUTHOR

Anna Glynn is a speaker, author, trainer and coach. Having worked in the corporate sector for over a decade, including leading sales teams, Anna is passionate about translating the latest research into practical strategies for sales leaders that support themselves, their teams and their organisations to thrive.

Anna understands what it's like to manage people and be responsible for driving growth in the workplace. During her time in management, Anna started implementing what she learned from her studies and saw first-hand the positive impacts on her team. So, she has walked what she talks.

In her practice, Anna has worked with global businesses across a range of industries. And the results she has achieved with her clients are impressive.

Anna has been interviewed for podcasts and radio and writes a regular blog called 'For What It's Worth'. Anna holds a Masters in Applied Positive Psychology (First Class Honours) and a Graduate Certificate in Positive Psychology (First Class Honours) from the University of Melbourne, a Bachelor of Commerce and a Bachelor of Arts from Monash University.

Anna's mission is to create workplaces where people are at their best each day and are better off for having worked there.

You can find out more about Anna and her work at:

www.annaglynn.com.au or
www.linkedin.com/in/anna-glynn-mapp-0797b639/

ENDNOTES

Introduction

1. Pink, D.H. (2013). *To Sell is Human: The surprising truth about moving others*. Riverhead Books.

Chapter One

1. Development Dimensions International. (2023). *Global leadership forecast series CEO leadership report 2023*.

2. PricewaterhouseCoopers. (2022). *PwC Australia's 25th CEO survey, onwards and upwards: The most important problems Australia's CEOs are solving for growth today and tomorrow*.

3. Hrehocik, M. (2007). The best sales force. *Sales and Marketing Management, 159*(8), 22–27.

4. Schaufeli, W. B., & Bakker, A. B. (2004). Job demands, job resources, and their relationship with burnout and engagement: A multi-sample study. *Journal of Organizational Behavior, 25*(3), 293–315.

5. Gallup. (2023). *State of the global workplace 2023 report*.

6. Pendell, R. (2022, June 14). *Employee engagement strategies: Fixing the World's $8.8 trillion problem*. Gallup.

7. Bakker, A. B., Schaufeli, W. B., Leiter, M. P., & Taris, T. W. (2008). Work engagement: An emerging concept in occupational health psychology. *Work & Stress, 22*(3), 187–200.

8. Harter, J., & Adkins, A. (2015). What great managers do to engage employees. *Harvard Business Review, 64.*

9. PricewaterhouseCoopers. (2021). *The Future of Work. What workers want: Winning the war for talent.*

10. Gallup. (2023). *State of the Global Workplace 2023 Report.*

11. Association of Talent Development. (2023). *State of Sales Training.*

12. Cespedes F. V., & Lee, Y. (2017). Your sales training is probably lacklustre. Here's how to fix it. *Harvard Business Review.*

13. Barrett, S. (2018). *The history of sales methodologies – Why some work and others don't.* Whitepaper.

14. Ibid.

Chapter Two

1. Kurniawati, D. T., & Izza, N. A. (2022). Leadership effectiveness as a predictor of turnover intention: Determinants of work stress. *International Journal of Research in Business and Social Science,* (2147- 4478), *11*(9), 131-139.

Chapter Three

1. Dubreuil, P., Forest, J., Gillet, N., Fernet, C., Thibault-Landry, A., Crevier-Braud, L., & Girouard, S. (2016). Facilitating well-being and performance through the development of strengths at work: Results from an intervention program. *International Journal of Applied Positive Psychology, 1*(1-3), 1-19.

2. Van Woerkom, M., & Meyers, M. C. (2015). My strengths count! Effects of a strengths-based psychological climate on positive affect and job performance. *Human Resource Management, 54*(1), 81-103.

3. Clark, T. R. (2020). *The 4 Stages of Psychological Safety: Defining the path to inclusion and innovation.* Berrett-Koehler Publishers.

4. Delizonna, L. (2017). High-performing teams need psychological safety. Here's how to create it. *Harvard Business Review, 8*, 1-5.

5. Edmondson, A. (1999). Psychological safety and learning behavior in work teams. *Administrative Science Quarterly, 44*(2), 350-383.

6. Avey, J. B., Wernsing, T. S., & Mhatre, K. H. (2011). A longitudinal analysis of positive psychological constructs and emotions on stress, anxiety, and well-being. *Journal of Leadership & Organizational Studies, 18*(2), 216-228.

7. Seligman, M. E., & Schulman, P. (1986). Explanatory style as a predictor of productivity and quitting among life insurance sales agents. *Journal of Personality and Social Psychology, 50*(4), 832.

8. Seligman, M. E. (2011). *Flourish: A visionary new understanding of happiness and well-being.* Simon & Schuster.

9. Dutton, J. E., & Spreitzer, G. M. (2014). *How to be a Positive Leader: Small actions, big impact.* Berrett-Koehler Publishers.

10. Stephens, J. P., Heaphy, E., & Dutton, J. E. (2011). High-quality connections. In G. M. Spreitzer & K. S. Cameron

(Eds.), *The Oxford handbook of positive organizational scholarship*, (pp. 385-399). Oxford University Press.

11. Ryan, R. M., & Deci, E. L. (2000). Self-determination theory and the facilitation of intrinsic motivation, social development, and well-being. *American Psychologist, 55*(1), 68.

12. Steger, M. F. (2016). Creating meaning and purpose at work. In L. G. Oades, M. F. Steger, D. A. Fave, & J. Passmore (Eds.), *The Wiley Blackwell handbook of the psychology of positivity and strengths-based approaches at work*, (pp. 60-81). John Wiley & Sons.

Chapter Four

1. Cooperrider, D. L., & McQuaid, M. (2012). The positive arc of systemic strengths: How appreciative inquiry and sustainable designing can bring out the best in human systems. *Journal of Corporate Citizenship*, (46), 71-102.

2. Linley, P. A. (2008). *Average to A+: Realising strengths in yourself and others*. CAPP Press.

3. Buckingham, M., & Clifton, D. O. (2001). *Now, Discover Your Strengths*. Free Press.

4. Bakker, A. B., Hetland, J., Olsen, O. K., & Espevik, R. (2019). Daily strengths use and employee well-being: The moderating role of personality. *Journal of Occupational and Organizational Psychology, 92*(1), 144-168.

5. Dubreuil, P., Forest, J., Gillet, N., Fernet, C., Thibault-Landry, A., Crevier-Braud, L., & Girouard, S. (2016). Facilitating well-being and performance through the development of strengths at work: Results from an

intervention program. *International Journal of Applied Positive Psychology*, *1*(1-3), 1-19.

6. Govindji, R., & Linley, P. A. (2007). Strengths use, self-concordance and well-being: Implications for strengths coaching and coaching psychologists. *International Coaching Psychology Review*, *2*(2), 143-153.

7. Hill, J. (2001, April). *How well do we know our strengths?* Paper presented at the British Psychological Society Centenary Conference, Glasgow.

8. Bakker, A. B., Hetland, J., Olsen, O. K., & Espevik, R. (2019). Daily strengths use and employee well-being: The moderating role of personality. *Journal of Occupational and Organizational Psychology*, *92*(1), 144-168.

9. Linley, P. A., Nielsen, K. M., Gillett, R., & Biswas-Diener, R. (2010). Using signature strengths in pursuit of goals: Effects on goal progress, need satisfaction, and well-being, and implications for coaching psychologists. *International Coaching Psychology Review*, *5*(1), 6-15.

10. Corporate Leadership Council. (2004). *Driving performance and retention through employee engagement*. Washington, DC: Corporate Executive Board.

11. Govindji, R., & Linley, P. A. (2007). Strengths use, self-concordance and well-being: Implications for strengths coaching and coaching psychologists. *International Coaching Psychology Review*, *2*(2), 143-153.

12. Gallup. (2023). *State of the Global Workplace 2023 Report*.

13. Matthews, L. M., Zablah, A. R., Hair, J. F., & Marshall, G. W. (2016). Increased engagement or reduced exhaustion: Which accounts for the effect of job resources on

salesperson job outcomes? *Journal of Marketing Theory and Practice, 24*(3), 249–264.

14. Schaufeli, W. B., & Bakker, A. B. (2004). Job demands, job resources, and their relationship with burnout and engagement: A multi-sample study. *Journal of Organizational Behavior: The International Journal of Industrial, Occupational and Organizational Psychology and Behavior, 25*(3), 293-315.

15. Csikszentmihalyi, M. (2008). *Flow: The psychology of optimal experience.* Harper Perennial.

16. Wrzesniewski, A., & Dutton, J. E. (2001). Crafting a job: Revisioning employees as active crafters of their work. *Academy of Management Review, 26*(2), 179-201.

Chapter Five

1. Brockner, J., Siegel, P. A., Daly, J. P., Tyler, T., & Martin, C. (1997). When trust matters: The moderating effect of outcome favorability. *Administrative Science Quarterly*, 558-583.

2. Sinek, S. (2014). *Leaders Eat Last: Why some teams pull together and others don't.* Penguin.

3. Edmondson, A. C. (2018). *The Fearless Organization: Creating psychological safety in the workplace for learning, innovation, and growth.* John Wiley & Sons.

4. McQuaid, M., & Williams, P. (2023). *Your Leadership Blueprint: Fostering psychosocial safety at work.* Michelle McQuaid.

5. Edmondson, A. C., & Lei, Z. (2014). Psychological safety: The history, renaissance, and future of an interpersonal

construct. *Annual Review of Organisational Psychology and Organisational Behavior, 1*(1), 23-43.

6. Duhigg, C. (2016). What Google learned from its quest to build the perfect team. *The New York Times Magazine, 26.*

7. May, D. R., Gilson, R. L., & Harter, L. M. (2004). The psychological conditions of meaningfulness, safety and availability and the engagement of the human spirit at work. *Journal of Occupational and Organizational Psychology, 77*(1), 11-37.

8. McQuaid, M., & Melville, R. (2019). *The Learning Loop.*

Chapter Six

1. Masten A. S., Powell J. L., & Luthar S. S. (2003). A resilience framework for research, policy, and practice. In S. S. Luthar (Ed.), *Resilience and Vulnerability: Adaptation in the context of childhood adversities*, (pp. 1-28). Cambridge University Press.

2. Hone, L. (2017). *Resilient Grieving: Finding strength and embracing life after a loss that changes everything.* The Experiment.

3. World Health Organization. (2019). *Burn-out an occupational phenomenon: International classification of diseases.*

4. Killingsworth, M. A., & Gilbert, D. T. (2010). A wandering mind is an unhappy mind. *Science, 330*(6006), 932-932.

5. Rotter, J. (1966). Generalized expectancies for internal versus external control of reinforcement. *Psychological Monographs, 80*(1), 1–28.

6. Covey, S. R. (2020). *The 7 Habits of Highly Effective People.* Simon & Schuster.

7. Fredrickson, B. L. (2001). The role of positive emotions in positive psychology: The broaden-and-build theory of positive emotions. *American Psychologist, 56*(3), 218–226.

8. Losada, M., & Heaphy, E. (2004). The role of positivity and connectivity in the performance of business teams. *American Behavioral Scientist, 47*(6), 740-765.

9. O'Neill, O. M. (2021). Emotional culture and the angry team. In A. B. Adler & D. Forbes (Eds.), *Anger at work: prevention, intervention, and treatment in high-risk occupations,* (pp. 111–140). American Psychological Association.

10. Barsade, S. G. (2002). The ripple effect: Emotional contagion and its influence on group behavior. *Administrative Science Quarterly, 47*(4), 644-675.

11. Nagoski, E., & Nagoski, D. M. A. (2020). *Burnout: The secret to unlocking the stress cycle.* Ballantine Books.

Chapter Seven

1. Schulman, P. (1999). Applying learned optimism to increase sales productivity. *Journal of Personal Selling & Sales Management, 19*(1), 31-37.

2. Ibid.

3. Carver, C. S., Scheier, M. F., & Segerstrom, S. C. (2010). Optimism. *Clinical Psychology Review, 30*(7), 879-889.

4. Kaniel, R., Massey, C., & Robinson, D. T. (2010, July 21). Optimism and economic crisis. Available at http://dx.doi.org/10.2139/ssrn.1579050.

5. Seligman, M. E. (2011). *Flourish: A visionary new understanding of happiness and well-being.* Simon & Schuster.

6. Dweck, C. (2017). *Mindset: Changing the way you think to fulfil your potential.* Hachette UK.

7. Diener, E., & Chan, M. Y. (2011). Happy people live longer: Subjective well-being contributes to health and longevity. *Applied Psychology: Health and Well-Being, 3*(1), 1-43.

Chapter Eight

1. Cross, R., & Thomas, R. J. (2011). Managing yourself: A smarter way to network. *Harvard Business Review.* July – August.

2. Dutton, J. E. (2014). Build high-quality connections. In J. E. Dutton & G.M. Spreitzer (Eds.), *How to be a Positive Leader: Small actions, big impact.* (pp. 11-22). Berrett-Koehler Publishers.

3. Lencioni, P. (2002). *The Five Dysfunctions of a Team.* John Wiley & Sons.

4. Patel, A., & Plowman, S. (2022). The increasing importance of a best friend at work. *Gallup.*

5. Bellet, C. S., De Neve, J. E., & Ward, G. (2023). Does employee happiness have an impact on productivity? *Management Science.*

6. Fredrickson, B. L. (2001). The role of positive emotions in positive psychology: The broaden-and-build theory of positive emotions. *American Psychologist, 56*(3), 218–226.

7. Nagoski, E., & Amelia Nagoski, D. M. A. (2020). *Burnout: The secret to unlocking the stress cycle.* Ballantine Books.

8. The Wellbeing Lab. (2021). *The State of Wellbeing in Australian Workplaces. The Wellbeing Lab 2019-2021 Workplace Report.*

9. Porath, C., & Pearson, C. (2013). The price of incivility. *Harvard Business Review, 91*(1-2), 114-121.

10. Sunder, S., Kumar, V., Goreczny, A., & Maurer, T. (2017). Why do salespeople quit? An empirical examination of own and peer effects on salesperson turnover behavior. *Journal of Marketing Research, 54*(3), 381-397.

11. Porath, C., & Pearson, C. (2013). The price of incivility. *Harvard Business Review, 91*(1-2), 114-121.

12. Rosales, R. (2015). Energizing social interactions at work: An exploration of relationships that generate employee and organizational thriving. *Open Journal of Social Sciences.* 4.

13. Dutton, J. E. (2014). Build high-quality connections. In J. E. Dutton & G.M. Spreitzer (Eds.), *How to be a Positive Leader: Small actions, big impact.* (pp. 11-22). Berrett-Koehler Publishers.

14. Brown, B. (2015). *Rising Strong: The reckoning. The rumble. The revolution.* Random House.

Chapter Nine

1. Diamond, D. (2013). Just 8% of people achieve their New Year's resolutions. Here's how they do it. *Forbes.*

2. Ryan, R. M., & Deci, E. L. (2000). Self-determination theory and the facilitation of intrinsic motivation, social development, and well-being. *American Psychologist, 55,* 68–78.

3. Ibid.

4. Chalofsky, N., & Krishna, V. (2009). Meaningfulness, commitment, and engagement: The intersection of a deeper level of intrinsic motivation. *Advances in Developing Human Resources, 11*(2), 189-203.

5. Ryan, R. M., & Deci, E. L. (2000). Self-determination theory and the facilitation of intrinsic motivation, social development, and well-being. *American Psychologist, 55,* 68–78.

6. Frankl, V. E. (1985). *Man's Search for Meaning.* Simon & Schuster.

Chapter Ten

1. Lyubomirsky, S. (2008). *The How of Happiness: A practical guide to getting the life you want.* Penguin.

2. Fogg, B. J. (2019). *Tiny Habits: The small changes that change everything.* Eamon Dolan Books.

3. Neal, D. T., Wood, W., & Quinn, J. M. (2006). Habits – a repeat performance. *Current Directions in Psychological Science, 15*(4), 198-202.

4. Clear, J. (2018). *Atomic Habits.* Random House.

5. Fogg, B. J. (2019). *Tiny Habits: The small changes that change everything.* Eamon Dolan Books.

6. Duhigg, C. (2013). *The Power of Habit: Why we do what we do and how to change.* Random House.

7. Neff, K. (2023). What is self-compassion? https://selfcompassion.org/the-three-elements-of-self-compassion-2/

8. McQuaid, M., & Melville, R. (2019). *The Learning Loop.*

Chapter Eleven

1. Jarden, A. (2015). Introducing workplace wellbeing to organizations: The "Me, We, Us" model. *Positive Work and Organizations: Research and Practice*, December(1).